ALONG THE WAY AN 11 DAY WALK IN JAPAN 1992

SEA LEVEL WATERLINE   DEATH VALLEY CALIFORNIA 1982

RICHARD LONG

WALKING THE LINE

Thames & Hudson

A LINE IN THE HIMALAYAS

1975

CONTENTS

ARIZONA 1970

(A BOOT-HEEL LINE)

FOREWORD

Richard Long is not an artist who works in a studio. In fact I doubt if he has ever had a proper studio. Generally speaking the only art-related work he does in his house is the layouts for the printer of his text pieces, some hand-written lettering and the paper work necessary for his very organised, much-travelled life. All his major works are made in museums and galleries, or in the countryside, in the solitude of the wild places of the world, or while walking along its inhabited, though often unpeopled areas, on roads and footpaths. He has different rationales for doing different things. Walking in landscape or working in a museum, each has its own set of parameters.

Long chooses to work with landscape because since childhood he always has, and because it gives him the most pleasure and the greatest inspiration. In the nineteen-sixties, when he started out on this road, the prevailing climate in the art world was urban, and indeed nearly forty years later it still is. Not only were the possibilities landscape had to offer then generally ignored, there is still no one today who comes remotely near Long's capabilities as a sculptor in the modernist tradition working with landscape or, perhaps one should say more properly, with the surface of the earth.

By the late sixties when Richard Long left St Martin's School of Art he was already recognised internationally as a leading figure of the avant garde. Since then he has produced an astonishing body of work for literally hundreds of exhibitions around the world. Although his first circles and lines directly marking the surface of the earth were undertaken in an intuitive spirit rather than an awareness of their implications, from then on it became clear to him that the 'whole world was open to work with', and that here was something he would be using for the rest of his life. The circle of turf in a Bristol garden, the line of footsteps flattening the grass in a local field, initiated a journey of consciousness peculiarly suited to the general growing understanding of the planet as a whole and as part of a greater cosmos. His is a point of view that is both timeless and also makes a great deal of sense in the world of planes and rockets and scientific discoveries, where the frontiers of space and time have been extended as never before.

The structure of Long's sculpture is based in part on the living reality of the situation in which it is created (the earth itself or substances derived from it) in all its complexity and detail. It is also partly based on a simple abstract formal geometry of lines and circles and their variants (arcs, ellipses, spirals, zigzags, meanders etc). The artist's use of geometry and of time and distance is balanced against the world as he finds it and the accidents of chance. Kicking stones to form a line, for example, is different from placing them in a line, and also enjoyable in a different way. Every stone and its response to movement in whatever manner or place is different. The artist plays his part and nature plays hers. As Long has so often been quoted as saying 'it's the touching and the meaning of the touching that matters'. The mutual respect achieved through this kind of sacred conversation with the land allows him to reveal to us aspects of the world which would otherwise be invisible.

His text works 'feed the imagination' and his wall and floor pieces 'feed the senses'. In every case the work of art extends 'as far as the eye can see'. This operates both visually and figuratively. Visually a work made on the ground at a stopping place along a walk also includes everything around it, but the choices the artist makes, and the things he takes into account, extend beyond the visual into the realms of ideas, movement, time, knowledge, measurement, mathematics, memory and so on.

The beauty in Long's work lies in equal part in the formal structure of his ideas and in the aesthetic pleasure offered by the materials he uses, or the spectacular views of nature documented by his photographs. Yet it is as much to do with perception as that of any artist of the past. He sees through the outward appearance of his subject while taking into account every aspect of its existence.

Long has always been conscious that he is part of a moving world. He demonstrates how everything from the smallest to the largest element, including the artist himself, is in a state of continuous and relative motion. This is also something he has enjoyed observing since childhood, and he studied Einstein's Theory of Relativity at art college. Even his use of lines and circles is part of it, the former signifying movement forward, the latter a stopping point in the midst of motion. Movement of the planets, seasons, tides and winds among other things are frequent subjects. It clearly gives him special pleasure to turn cosmic events to his own advantage, as in a walk by the light of the full moon on the longest night of the year – a particular year.

In one of his most poignant and romantic early works, *Reflections in Little Pigeon River, Great Smokey Mountains, Tennessee*, 1970, Richard Long gives an unforgettable insight into his use of lines. At the bottom of the photograph he quotes a verse from a song by Johnny Cash, the country and western singer:

'I keep a close watch on this heart of mine
I keep my eyes wide open all the time
I keep the ends out for the tie that binds
Because you're mine
I walk the line'

The photograph shows a cross made by rearranging the stones beneath the water on the bed of a shallow river overhung with trees. The lines meet and fuse, the stream flows on regardless. Eventually it will wash away the traces of this conjunction.

Our world is made up of lines, from comet tails to DNA. Everything is connected. Everything is sequential. Everything that moves, from a snail to a lava flow, leaves a line, a trace of its passing. A line can be fate, a commitment, a fact, a relationship, a place. Some lines are well trodden paths, some intersect, some pass at a distance, some return to their origins. We all walk the line. We have an end and a beginning which is joined to a much longer invisible line in the past and in the future.

Long's touch has always been famously light. Unlike some land artists, he has never made permanent changes to the land or moved great quantities of earth. After photographing them he often prefers to stand down the stones he has made into a circle. But over the years, as museums have offered him increasingly grand exhibition opportunities, he has created more and more pieces on a spectacularly large scale, often tens of metres in height or length. Since the early nineteen-eighties many have been mud works made generally on museum and gallery walls (though sometimes also on the floor).

For these Long uses his hand dipped in mud, it could be River Avon mud from the river that flows through his home town of Bristol, or another similar substance appropriate to the site, such as china clay in Cornwall, or possibly both. Although he works at speed directly on the wall (which could be painted black or white) these are not to be regarded as paintings. They are created from the same kind of conjunction between the substance of the mud, the energy of the artist and the spatial situation, as his stone floor pieces or his interventions in the landscape. He is simply touching the world in a different way, working with a vertical surface and a more fluid substance, which demands a different kind of virtuosity to handle both the geometry and the accidents of the natural material. Just as every stone is different, every splash of mud is different and eloquent of its origin and purpose and the speed with which it strikes the surface of the wall. Though spectacularly beautiful, like fireworks or flowers, whereas Long's floor sculptures can be re-created indefinitely by others according to the artist's instructions, the mud works are inherently ephemeral: only the artist can make them. So where they cannot be preserved, photographs alone remain to remind us of the phenomena of past exhibitions.

To keep such a record is part of the purpose of this book. *Walking the Line* is a companion to *Walking in Circles* published in 1991. It includes almost three hundred works mostly made since that date. It is not a catalogue raisonné, though on the way to being one. And as in the case of the previous volume the book has been laid out by the artist in his inimitable style, so that turning the pages is an adventure itself.

Walking the Line is a unique primary source of information on the career of one of the greatest living artists. As well as a selection of revealing and amusing extracts from the artist's notebooks and diaries (all previously unpublished), it also includes the fine essay by Paul Moorhouse, published by Tate St Ives earlier this year, which we are delighted to reproduce. Additionally the biographical, bibliographical and exhibition history, which Gerard Vermeulen of the Richard Long Newsletter in Nijmegen has been compiling for some years, appears here, as work in progress, for the first time. We are grateful to both of them for their permission to use this material. Special thanks and acknowledgment go above all to the designer, Herman Lelie who has coordinated the project from the beginning, and to Stefania Bonelli for her assistance. We particularly also wish to thank Francis Atterbury, Guido de Werd and his team at Kleve, Karsten Schubert, Denise Hooker, Linda Saunders, Galerie Tschudi, Tucci Russo, Studio per l'Arte Contemporanea, the James Cohan Gallery, Sperone Westwater and the Konrad Fischer Galerie.

AS

SNOW STONES
A SIX DAY WALK IN THE SWISS ALPS 2002

A LINE IN IRELAND
1974

BRUSHED PATH A LINE IN NEPAL

ALONG A 21 DAY WALK 1983

SHIRAKAMI LINE
AN 8 DAY WALK IN AOMORI JAPAN 1997

WALKING A LINE THROUGH LEAVES
ALONG AN 8 DAY MOUNTAIN WALK IN SOBAEKSAN
KOREA SPRING 1993

17

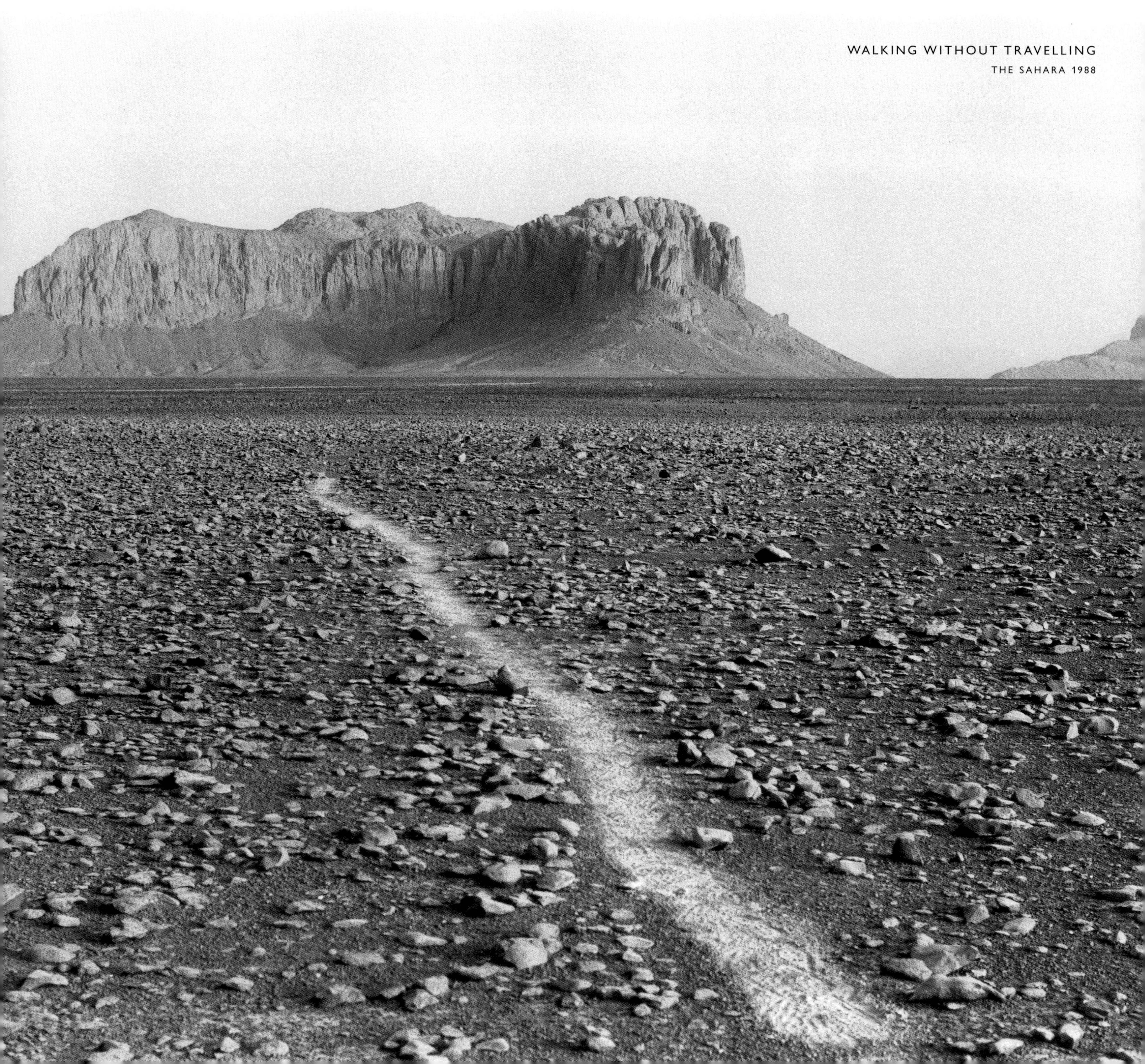

WALKING WITHOUT TRAVELLING

THE SAHARA 1988

WEST EAST LINE

WALKING A LINE ON BURNT HEATHER

ALONG AN 8 DAY WALK OF 187 MILES FROM THE WEST COAST TO THE EAST COAST OF SCOTLAND

1991

CLOUDS

IN THE CLOUD

ALONG AN 8 DAY WALK ACROSS SCOTLAND

3/4 HOUR IN CLOUD

WHILE GOING OVER BEN MACDUI

THE HIGHEST POINT OF THE WALK

COAST TO COAST WEST TO EAST 1991

A CLOUDLESS WALK

AN EASTWARD WALK OF 121 MILES IN 3$^{1}/_{2}$ DAYS
FROM THE MOUTH OF THE LOIRE TO THE FIRST CLOUD

FRANCE 1995

CLOUD CIRCLE

AN EIGHT DAY WALK IN THE SOUTH TYROL

ITALY 1996

A CLOUDY WALK

DURING A WALK OF 7 DAYS ACROSS IRELAND
1½ HOURS OF SUNSHINE

FROM THE WEST COAST TO THE EAST COAST WINTER 1998

A DAY'S WALK ACROSS DARTMOOR
FOLLOWING THE DRIFT OF THE CLOUDS

THE INTRICACY OF THE SKEIN, THE COMPLEXITY OF THE WEB: RICHARD LONG'S ART

Paul Moorhouse

> *Always think of the universe as one living organism, with a single substance*
> *and a single soul; and observe how all things are submitted to the single*
> *perceptivity of this one whole, all are moved by its single impulse, and all*
> *play their part in the causation of every event that happens. Remark the*
> *intricacy of the skein, the complexity of the web.*
> (Marcus Aurelius, *Meditations*)[1]

In 1987 Richard Long made a work of art involving two stones. The size, shape and colour of these objects is not recorded but undoubtedly they were small enough to be held in the hand and light enough to be carried. At a certain, unspecified moment in that particular year, Long stood on the beach at Aldeburgh on the English east coast and, from the millions of similar pebbles there, he selected the first stone. He then set out on a journey, carrying this modest, natural relic of the Suffolk landscape.

His destination was the beach at Aberystwyth on the Welsh west coast. He walked all the way, covering a distance of over 300 miles in around ten days. We are not told what he saw and felt during his journey. It appears, however, that when he reached his destination he placed the stone he had been carrying in these new surroundings. He then picked up a different stone and reversed the process, taking it with him as he commenced the walk back to Aldeburgh. Whether he used the same route is not divulged. On his arrival at the east coast, twenty days after he last stood there, he placed the stone he had carried from Aberystwyth on the beach at Aldeburgh. Some time after the completion of the walk he then made a framed text work – *Crossing Stones* – which provides a succinct description of this activity.

It is now fifteen years since Long carried out this walk and almost certainly the two stones are no longer exactly where he left them. The weather, the tides, and endless natural movement in the landscape will have ensured that nothing at either place will have remained the same. In placing the stones Long created a fragile structure which has presumably disappeared; or, rather, it has simply returned to nature. Nevertheless, somewhere at Aldeburgh and Aberystwyth, these two stones are almost certainly still there: transplanted and assimilated; endlessly buried, exposed and covered over again by the elements; each moving imperceptibly in the orbit of their radically altered situation. For what *is* certain is the significance that Long's intervention has had for the natural order of things.

THROWING STONES INTO A LINE

A SIX DAY WALK IN THE ATLAS MOUNTAINS

MOROCCO 1979

A LINE IN BOLIVIA KICKED STONES

1981

Plucked from their former situation, the stones remain physically remote. Now, however, they are also intimately *connected* by the bonds of their shared condition. Both stones have made a unique crossing and the resulting connection between them exists in the context of the work of art which created this situation. A particular relationship between certain landscape elements has been defined by the power of an idea and its *actual* execution: nature touched lightly, yet articulated at the deepest levels. In the fertile interaction of these apparent opposites – a living human presence and the inert matter of the natural world – the intangible essence of Long's art may be glimpsed.

MOVING WORLD

In a career that now spans more than thirty-five years, Long has created a substantial and varied body of work in which the relationship between man and nature is a central, unifying concern. Taking nature both as his subject and as the source of his materials, Long's artistic ethos has always been one of direct, dynamic, physical involvement with landscape. This is evident in his earliest works, notably when in 1964 he made a drawing on the ground on the Bristol Downs simply by rolling a snowball across the snow-covered grass. The notion of impermanence entailed by this work has been an abiding principle in his subsequent interactions with nature. It was, however, the decision he took in 1967 to make sculpture out of walking which established the principal defining characteristic of Long's art and the course it has followed to the present day.

Long's first walking piece, *Ben Nevis Hitch-Hike* 1967 comprised a six-day walking and hitch-hiking journey from London to the summit of Ben Nevis and back. As shown in the related map work which provides a record of Long's route and itinerary, during the course of this trip a photograph was taken at each of six locations, each unnamed location being specified on an outline map of Britain by the day the photograph was taken. Even today, in a visual culture long accustomed to art being made from any material whatsoever, including pre-existing objects, there is something about a sculpture being made out of a *walk* which still challenges some deeply held assumptions. Most firmly rooted among these is, perhaps, the sense that – no matter what it is made of – a sculpture should at least have a physical form or attributes that can be perceived. From the outset, walking as art confounded such expectations. Since then, Long's innovations have been widely embraced as a radical redefining of the boundaries of sculpture. But, even so, it is still pertinent – and illuminating – to ask: in what sense *can* a walk be a sculpture? Indeed, how does a walk function as a work of art at all?

Part of the difficulty of accounting for such developments is that they cannot easily be accommodated within recognised art historical theories and categories. Duchamp's designation of pre-fabricated objects as works of art is the source of a major tributary running through Modernism. It has, however, limited relevance to an appreciation of Long's designation of walking as art. Duchamp's innovation – bold as it was – rests on the perception of one or more physical objects. In contrast, Long took sculpture into the domain of the immaterial: the walk comprises the movement of a body through time and space and, as such, has no permanent physical attributes. Nor can the walk as artwork be understood by reference to avant-garde art movements such as Conceptual Art, whose emergence formed the backdrop to Long's own artistic development. The premium placed by conceptual artists on ideas – to the extent that their actual realisation is secondary – is completely antithetical to Long. As in the example of *Crossing Stones*, the walk itself may have no lasting physical attributes but the work could not exist if the walk had not happened.

Other approaches to these questions are needed and Long himself has provided insights. He has observed: 'Walking itself has a cultural history, from Pilgrims to the wandering Japanese poets, the English Romantics and contemporary long-distance walkers.'[2] Walking is a fundamental, universal activity, the basis of locomotion through the world for human beings. But as well as being essentially practical, as Long implies it is also closely bound up with the cultures of different races throughout the ages. Though its principal function is movement, people do not only walk to get from one place to another. Walking is a way of engaging and interacting with the world, providing the means of exposing oneself to new, changing perceptions and experiences and of acquiring an expanded awareness of our surroundings. Through such experiences, and through a deeper understanding of the places we occupy, we acquire a better understanding of our own position in the world.

Such considerations are germane to an understanding of the importance of walking in Long's art. For example, the subject of *Walking in a Moving World*, a recent text work, is relativity. It describes a five-day walk undertaken by Long in Powys in 2001. It does so in terms of the artist's different physical relationships with various natural phenomena as he moves across the landscape. The text is arranged by listing these phenomena in order of the speeds at which *they* are moving, from fastest to slowest – from fleeting cloud shadows to an imperceptibly slow glacial boulder moving at geological speed. The impression conveyed is of a world in movement, never still. There is a vivid sense of *relation* between the walker's movements and his changing surroundings through the use of particular phrases – *between*, *into*, *across*, *through*, *under* and *over* – words which only have meaning in relative terms. In these ways, the underlying subject of the work is revealed: through walking the intimate connection between man and nature is revealed.

GOBI DESERT CIRCLE

MONGOLIA 1996

WALKING IN A MOVING WORLD

BETWEEN CLOUD SHADOWS

INTO A HEADWIND

ACROSS A RIVER

THROUGH SPRING BRACKEN

UNDER A BEECH TREE

OVER A GLACIAL BOULDER

A 5 DAY WALK IN POWYS 2001

35

In Long's art, the walk is thus the most direct, immediate and practical way of interacting with nature. It would however be wrong to assume that this universal activity has, in an unqualified way, simply been redesignated as art. As *Crossing Stones* and *Walking in a Moving World* both demonstrate, Long's walks are considered and structured. They have a sense of purpose and a definite character. Each walk is structured so that different elements become connected and drawn into perceivable relationships. Sometimes these connections are relatively simple. In an early work such as *A Ten Mile Walk* 1968, for example, Long walked for ten miles in a straight line. As a result, distance and direction were linked. In turn, from the relationship drawn between those two properties, two specific places – the start and finish of the walk – became connected, as did all the unnamed points traversed during the walk. The walk has a structure which the related mapwork makes explicit and which the viewer can experience imaginatively.

Other walks are more complex, making subtle connections between abstract properties of time, distance, speed of walking and perception in addition to the linking of particular geographical points. These developments are evident in a walk made on Dartmoor in 1970: *For six consecutive nights I walked by compass, from east to west, the line drawn on the map. The time taken was recorded at the end of each walk.* Walking in darkness, Long paced out precisely the same route on six nights in succession. Using a compass to determine his direction, he timed himself on each occasion, noting that overall his walking time became shorter as his familiarity with the landscape at night grew and his speed increased. The walk is structured in terms of the relationships created between the artist's body, his experiences, aspects of the landscapes – and time. That the walk defines certain relationships locates it within the language used in speaking of sculpture. That these relationships do not have a material form shows Long's achievement in taking the definition of sculpture beyond the making of objects.

FOLLOWING AN IDEA

The relationship between the idea for a walk, the walk itself, and the physical evidence of the walk, is a fundamental issue in Long's art. While it is possible to identify these different components singly, it is the interaction of these components that provides the fabric of his work. It is for this reason that, as already seen, Long's art falls outside the definition of Conceptual art. The idea is vital in that it defines the structure for a walk. But the walk is equally important in that it realises the idea, actualising the structure as physical movement through time and space, so that the work of art has a *real* – if transient – existence.

The walk's lack of permanence is intimately bound up with its subject. Nature is synonymous with movement and change. In providing a vehicle for exploring these issues, it is appropriate that the walk should be in harmony with them, providing a way of making art that is also impermanent. Nevertheless, nature also shows some evidence of the changes which galvanise it, even if some of these changes are recognisable only through a microscope. It is clear, therefore, that from the beginning, Long considered how the focus of his work – the walk – might leave a trace on the surface of the land.

His first such work was *A Line made by Walking* 1967. In keeping with his ethos of using means which are direct, immediate and practical, this took the form of a straight line running across a grass field: the result of repeating his steps. He then photographed the work. Simple to make and easy to describe, the implications of this piece were nevertheless profound. Essentially, its subject is the interaction of man and nature. Yet the way the work conveys this is economical, pure and appropriate. Without describing nature or adding anything superfluous, the work takes its place, temporarily, in nature – its subject and its means brought into perfect alignment. The principle of making a work of art about the meeting of man and nature by leaving a sign of that interaction is encapsulated in this work and in Long's subsequent development of that approach.

Since making *A Line made by Walking*, Long has made numerous other works which exist as impermanent traces of his walks, and of his physical presence in the landscape, at a range of sites and in various countries around the globe. In some cases, the connection between a walk and its physical consequences is overt. In *A Line of 164 Stones A Walk of 164 Miles* 1974, for example, Long walked across Ireland. During the course of his journey he stopped after every mile and placed a nearby stone on whichever road he was walking along. The resulting sculpture thus comprised 164 separate stones and spanned a distance of 164 miles – a sinuous, skein-like structure, from coast to coast, which tracked his movement across the landscape. In other works the connection with the walk is less obvious. Using stones, sticks, dust, mud, water – whatever is locally available – Long has made sculptures at certain points during the course of particular walks. These constructions belong to a restricted vocabulary of elemental shapes: lines, circles, spirals, crosses and ellipses. Sometimes they are formed by drawing together individual elements so that they form a shape. On other occasions, Long has removed elements – for example by kicking stones aside – to expose a shape on the surface of the ground.

Much has been made by commentators about the significance of these shapes. Allusions have been made to the way they echo forms in nature and also to their universal qualities in the way they cut across different cultures and periods. Such interpretations can certainly be accommodated within the broader context of Long's work. Arguably, however, the principal significance of these sculptures lies elsewhere. For example, in a work such as *1449 Stones at 1449 Feet*, a sculpture made on Dartmoor in 1979, there is little sense of any shape in particular. Instead, the stones are piled amorphously and it is their number and location that are important. As the title implies, the structure makes a connection between the precise number of stones that comprise the work and the exact height at which it is situated.

What this work has in common with those which are formally more pure – such as the circles or lines – is the way that both provide evidence of the artist's presence in a particular place. As with the walks, there is an inescapable sense of structure. This structure can exist in terms of the relationships drawn between invisible qualities of measurement, as in *1449 Stones at 1449 Feet*. Alternatively, the connections made can be physical and primarily visual, as in the grouping of stones in one of the circles. In both cases, what is pre-eminently significant is the fact of *arrangement*: the connecting of different elements. In Long's work, arrangement arises from the meeting of human characteristics with the natural materials of the world. As such it is an index – a trace – of the relation between man and nature.

The sculptures in the landscape are therefore a vital aspect of Long's art, making visible the relationship that is its central subject. To a large extent, however, these works are not seen by anyone apart from the artist and others who happen to come upon them. Not only are they temporary sculptures which begin the process of their assimilation back into nature as soon as the artist leaves them, they are also frequently in remote locations. In seeking to record the walks and sculptures, and to make them more widely visible, Long has adopted other strategies – in the form of maps, photographs and text – which can also be seen in terms of following, or providing the trace of, an idea.

Such strategies are apparent in Long's work almost from the beginning. For example, the track left by the snowball on Bristol Downs in 1964 was shortlived but the related photograph preserves a trace of this work's brief existence. Three years later – in *Ben Nevis Hitch Hike* 1967 – the walk was documented by photographs, a map and words used in combination. Long continued to use these elements in his subsequent work, sometimes independently, sometimes in different combinations. In Long's work, maps, photographs and words relate to a walk or sculpture as a footprint does to a foot. As signs, they are partial, revealing aspects of the experience that caused them; but they also provide – in their different ways – sufficient information for the viewer to *imagine* the circumstances which led to their creation.

This is most evident in the text works. Since 1977, Long has used words less as factual or descriptive annotations to photographs or maps and more as a discrete way of working in its own right. The role of the text works is to tell the story of individual walks. They take the form of words or phrases – notably observations, feelings, experiences, place-names, measurements of time, duration, number and distance – drawn into particular arrangements. They are, however, rarely constructed as narratives. Neither poetry nor straightforward prose, the structure of such texts is closer to sculpture than to literature, arising from the connection and interrelation of words, ideas and experiences. For example, *Walking to a Solar Eclipse* 1999, traces a walk in which destination, duration and distance are aligned with a certain momentary relationship between the sun, the moon and the earth. *Sunrise Circle* 1998 also evokes in words the meeting of a human gesture with certain natural forces: in this case the fleeting connection made between the rising of the sun and a hand drawing a circle in snow on a mountaintop in Ecuador.

In this way, the text works – like the photographs and maps – 'feed the imagination',[3] as Long puts it. They follow an idea, evoking its realisation as a walk or as a sculpture made during a walk. In the absence of these phenomena, words, cartographic symbols and images made with a camera are the traces that remain.

EARTH

The primary purpose of texts, maps and photographs is to document works which occur in the landscape, evoking that which is formless or remote. If their character is that of feeding the imagination, the works that Long makes specifically for display in a gallery space feed the senses. They have an immediate, tangible physical presence. The mud works are executed directly on a wall; the indoor sculptures use natural materials obtained locally. Both ways of working mirror Long's activities in the landscape. In the case of the sculpture, the connection between outdoor and indoor work is explicit. The mud works have no obvious counterpart in the landscape. This said, the use of mud connects directly with the works, using water alone, that Long makes in a natural setting. In a gallery space, mud makes the action of water and the rhythms of hand gestures visible and lasting. Mud is a natural bridge between water and stone, like fluid earth. Viewed in that light, a mud work – made rapidly and spontaneously – suggests a stone sculpture executed at lightning speed.

Some recent mud works have extended Long's engagement with ideas derived from Zen (the Japanese form of Buddhism) by introducing Chinese hexagrams as an underlying structure. In 2002 he made a work based on the I-Ching symbol for *Earth*.[4] As such, the medium for the work of art was aligned with its meaning. Taken from the earth, the mud work referred back to it. Echoing Chinese ideas about the reconciliation of opposites, the image existed – temporarily – as a record of impermanence: energy made visible, order imposed on chaos, a trace of the artist's direct involvement with his materials.

CIRCLE IN KOREA
ALONG AN 8 DAY MOUNTAIN WALK IN SOBAEKSAN KOREA 1993

BARK CIRCLE

As suggested by their splashes, drips and handmarks, mud works like *Earth* are made freely and gesturally. They are nevertheless underpinned by principles of arrangement and order. Like the stones and sticks used in the sculptures, inert matter is drawn into a complex pattern or system. A mud work by Long is a *constructed* thing: its cumulative handmarks echoing the individual steps in a walk or the separate stones that comprise a sculpture made in a landscape. The relationships between constituent parts are vital in each of these activities. But as *Earth* implies, in Long's work medium and meaning are closely interrelated. Beyond its formal characteristics, there lies a deeper significance.

Fundamental though the principle of arrangement is in Long's art, it is the singular character of the relationships created that carries meaning. In particular, the sense of *unity* expressed by these relationships is important. In the text work *River to River* 2001, a linking thread is drawn between three natural features – river, wood and tor – as the result of a walk on Dartmoor. The walk and the resulting text have imposed a pattern on these disparate elements. In another way, however, the work suggests that these natural features are *already* joined as part of an invisible and infinitely complex natural web. As such, the work of art is not just about imposing connections and order. Rather, there is a sense that it *reveals* a system of relationships: that it discloses a unity that already exists.

The idea of unified nature has antecedents in earlier art and philosophy. In the 19th century, the notion of the natural world – including man – as a single entity was a mainstay of Romantic thought. In *The Philosophy of Nature*, the influential German philosopher Schelling advanced the idea of nature evolving from matter into living things: plants, animals and humans. According to this view, everything is interrelated. The Romantic idea of the organic relation between man and nature has a resonance in Long's work. It would, however, be mistaken to overemphasise the affinity with Romanticism. Long's art does not foreground emotion or indulge in flights of the imagination. It is grounded instead in the direct experience of the real world. Also, whereas the Romantics stressed the primacy of the individual in perceiving and interpreting nature, Long's work draws man and nature into balance, proportion and equilibrium.

Rather, the sense of order, unity and harmony in Long's work is the product of an approach that is essentially rationalist. While its innovatory means of expression are embedded in the art of the late 20th century, its roots, if anything, are classical. In the ancient world, the relationship between man and nature was an abiding concern and the idea of order a passion. In Stoic philosophy, for example, human beings and nature were seen as the unified manifestation of the universal Mind. Consequently, the individual expressed his relationship with nature through the exercise of reason, which is a part of the universal Reason. As the Roman

Emperor Marcus Aurelius (AD 121–180), who was versed in Stoic philosophy, observed: 'an act that accords with nature is an act that accords with reason.'[5]

These principles find eloquent confirmation in Richard Long's art. Founded on a sense of deep accord with nature, his work expresses the beauty and fragility of this relationship. Involving direct interaction with nature and natural materials, its central means are rational and empirical. In the modern world, with a vastly expanded capacity for destruction, the relation of man and nature is as pressing and relevant as ever. For that reason, Long's art has a significance that is both timeless and universal.

This essay is a modified version of a text that was originally commissioned by Tate St Ives and which was first published in the catalogue for Richard Long's exhibition, *A Moving World*, held at Tate St Ives, July–October 2002.

Notes:
1 *Meditations,* Book Four, 40, trans. Maxwell Staniforth, London 1964, p 73
2 Artist's statement, 2000
3 Ibid
4 The work was made for Long's exhibition at Tate St Ives, July – October 2002
5 *Meditations,* Book Seven, 11, p 107

STONES

GRANITE LINE

SCATTERED ALONG A STRAIGHT 9 MILE LINE
223 STONES PLACED ON DARTMOOR

ENGLAND 1980

GRANITE STEPPING-STONE CIRCLE

A 5 MILE CIRCULAR WALK ON DARTMOOR
PASSING OVER 409 ROCK SLABS AND BOULDERS

ENGLAND 1980

STONE STEPS DAYS

FIRST DAY A STONE MOVED ONE STEP WEST
SECOND DAY THE STONE MOVED TWO STEPS NORTH
THIRD DAY THE STONE MOVED THREE STEPS EAST
FOURTH DAY THE STONE MOVED FOUR STEPS SOUTH
FIFTH DAY THE STONE MOVED FIVE STEPS WEST
SIXTH DAY THE STONE MOVED SIX STEPS NORTH
SEVENTH DAY THE STONE MOVED SEVEN STEPS EAST

LONGSTONE HILL

SOMERSET ENGLAND 1985

TWO SAHARA STONES

SITTING ON A MOUNTAINTOP
IN THE HOGGAR
CLAPPING TWO FLAT STONES TOGETHER
A THOUSAND TIMES

1988

HEAVIER   SLOWER   SHORTER
LIGHTER   FASTER   LONGER

A FOUR DAY WALK IN ENGLAND
PICKING A STONE UP EACH DAY AND CARRYING IT.
A FOUR DAY WALK IN WALES
SETTING DOWN ONE OF THE STONES EACH DAY.

1982

WIND STONES

LONG POINTED STONES

SCATTERED ALONG A 15 DAY WALK IN LAPPLAND
207 STONES TURNED TO POINT INTO THE WIND

1985

TEN STONES

A LONG SLOPE OF LAVA DUST ON A FLANK OF THE VOLCANO HEKLA

A LINE OF FIVE STONES SENT ROLLING DOWN IT IN 1974
A LINE OF FIVE STONES SENT ROLLING DOWN IT IN 1994

THE CROSSING PLACE OF TWO WALKS

ICELAND

EUROPE ASIA STONES

A LINE OF STONES DROPPED INTO THE WATER FROM WEST TO EAST ACROSS THE BOSPHORUS
A LINE OF STONES DROPPED INTO THE WATER FROM EAST TO WEST ACROSS THE BOSPHORUS

ISTANBUL TURKEY 1989

DOLOMITE STONES

STONES DROPPED INTO A CHASM
STONES PLACED IN A CIRCLE
STONES JAMMED INTO FISSURES
STONES THROWN TO HIT A ROCK
STONES SKIMMED ACROSS A SMALL LAKE
STONES THROWN OVER A PRECIPICE
TONES PLACED ON MOUNTAINTOP CAIRNS
STONES DISLODGED FROM THE PATH
STONES USED TO SECURE THE TENT
STONES THROWN INTO A CLOUD

CROSSING STONES

A STONE FROM ALDEBURGH BEACH ON THE EAST COAST CARRIED TO ABERYSTWYTH BEACH ON THE WEST COAST
A STONE FROM ABERYSTWYTH BEACH ON THE WEST COAST CARRIED TO ALDEBURGH BEACH ON THE EAST COAST

A 626 MILE WALK IN 20 DAYS

ENGLAND WALES ENGLAND

1987

AN EIGHT DAY WALK IN THE SOUTH TYROL

FANES PUEZ SELLA LANGKOFEL

ITALY 1996

TWO STONES

A STONE'S THROW FROM THE IRISH SEA TO A STONE'S THROW FROM THE NORTH SEA

A FOUR DAY WALK OF 122 MILES CROSSING THE LAKE DISTRICT AND THE PENNINES

WHITEHAVEN TO HARTLEPOOL

ENGLAND 1991

IN THE MIDDLE OF THE ROAD

HALFWAY STONE

IN THE MIDDLE OF THE WALK

A ROAD WALK OF 622 MILES IN 21 DAYS
FROM THE NORTH COAST TO THE SOUTH COAST OF SPAIN

RIBADESELLA TO MÁLAGA
1990

STONY GROUND

ALL IRELAND STONES

SEVENTH CAMP ALONG AN 8 DAY MOUNTAIN WALK IN SOBAEKSAN

A LINE OF 32 STONES RANDOMLY SPACED ALONG A WALKING LINE OF 382 MILES

THE TENT TETHERED WITH TWELVE FOOTPATH AND RIVERBANK STONES

A 12 DAY ROAD WALK FROM BALTIMORE BEACON ON THE SOUTH COAST
TO THE GIANT'S CAUSEWAY ON THE NORTH COAST

THE STONES LEFT IN THE SHAPE OF THE TENT

WINTER 1995

KOREA SPRING 1993

   小 白 山

DARTMOOR STONES

A STRAIGHT NORTHWARD WALK ACROSS DARTMOOR MOVING NINETY STONES EACH ONE STEP NORTH ALONG THE WAY

A STRAIGHT SOUTHWARD WALK ACROSS DARTMOOR MOVING NINETY STONES EACH ONE STEP SOUTH ALONG THE WAY

A STRAIGHT EASTWARD WALK ACROSS DARTMOOR MOVING NINETY STONES EACH ONE STEP EAST ALONG THE WAY

A STRAIGHT WESTWARD WALK ACROSS DARTMOOR MOVING NINETY STONES EACH ONE STEP WEST ALONG THE WAY

1992

STONES ON A CAIRN
DARTMOOR ENGLAND 1992

DARTMOOR CIRCLE

ALONG A TWO DAY WALK

1992

ROAD OF THREE CAIRNS

A CAIRN ON THE PAS DE PEYROL IN THE MASSIF CENTRAL AT 5190 FT.

A CAIRN ON THE COL DU LAUTARET IN THE FRENCH ALPS AT 6750 FT.

A CAIRN ON THE COLLE DI SESTRIERE IN THE ITALIAN ALPS AT 6668 FT.

THREE SMALL ROADSIDE CAIRNS BUILT ALONG A WALK OF 586 MILES IN 18½ DAYS FROM BORDEAUX TO TURIN

1992

WALK OF SEVEN CAIRNS

A CAIRN BUILT NEAR SHEEP BONES

A CAIRN BUILT AT A WINDY PLACE

A CAIRN BUILT WHERE A RAVEN FLEW OFF

A CAIRN BUILT ON THE FLOODLINE OF A RIVER

A CAIRN BUILT AFTER A ROLL OF THUNDER

A CAIRN BUILT AT MY CAMPSITE

A CAIRN BUILT IN A HAILSTORM

A FOUR DAY WALK IN THE BRECON BEACONS AND FFOREST FAWR

SOUTH WALES 1992

WALKING STONES

A WALK ACROSS ENGLAND FROM THE ATLANTIC OCEAN COAST TO THE NORTH SEA COAST

EACH DAY A STONE PICKED UP AND CARRIED FORWARD TO THE NEXT DAY
WHERE IT IS PUT DOWN AT THE PLACE OF THE NEXT STONE TO BE PICKED UP
AND SO ON FROM DAY TO DAY FROM STONE TO STONE

A WALK OF 382 MILES IN 11 DAYS
FROM A FIRST PEBBLE ON WELCOMBE MOUTH BEACH
TO THE LAST STONE THROWN INTO THE SEA AT LOWESTOFT

ENGLAND 1995

THE SAME THING
AT A DIFFERENT TIME
AT A DIFFERENT PLACE

A STONE BROUGHT FROM SOMEWHERE ON A PAST WALK
PLACED ON THE SUMMIT OF SNOWDON FOR A TIME DURING A FIVE DAY WALK IN NORTH WALES
AND CARRIED DOWN TO BE LEFT SOMEWHERE ON A FUTURE WALK

WINTER 1997

ALPINE STONES
NEAR THE POINTE DE LA PLAINE MORTE
A 13 DAY MOUNTAIN WALK BEGINNING AND ENDING IN LEUK
SWITZERLAND 2000

AN EXCHANGE OF STONES AT A PLACE FOR A TIME ON DARTMOOR

BRINGING A STONE FROM TIERRA DEL FUEGO
PLACING IT ON SADDLE TOR FOR THE DURATION OF A THREE DAY WALK AROUND DARTMOOR
AND REMOVING IT AT THE END OF THE WALK TO BE DROPPED INTO THE RIVER AVON IN BRISTOL

FINDING A STONE ON SADDLE TOR
CARRYING IT FOR THE DURATION OF A THREE DAY WALK AROUND DARTMOOR
AND RETURNING IT AT THE END OF THE WALK TO ITS PLACE ON SADDLE TOR

ENGLAND 1997

A ROLLING STONE

ALONG A 15 DAY WALK IN OREGON 2001

SPLASHING AROUND A CIRCLE

A STONE THROWN INTO EACH RIVER AND STREAM
AT ITS CROSSING PLACE WITH AN IMAGINARY CIRCLE 41 MILES WIDE
SURROUNDING SALISBURY PLAIN AND THE MARLBOROUGH DOWNS

A WALK OF FOUR DAYS ENGLAND 1997

SPLASH SPLASH SPLASH SPLASH SPLASH SPLASH SPLASH SPLASH SPLASH SPLASH SPLASH SPLASH SPLASH SPLASH SPLASH SPLASH SPLASH SPLASH SPLASH SPLASH

SPLASH
SPLASH

SPLASH

SPLASH

SPLASH

SPLASH

SPLASH

SPLASH

SPLASH

SPLASH

SPLASH

SPLASH
SPLASH

SPLASH

SPLASH
SPLASH

SPLASH

A LINE OF 33 STONES A WALK OF 33 DAYS

A STONE PLACED ON THE ROAD EACH DAY ALONG A WALK OF 1030 MILES IN 33 DAYS
FROM THE SOUTHERNMOST POINT TO THE NORTHERNMOST POINT OF MAINLAND BRITAIN

THE LIZARD TO DUNNET HEAD

1998

PASSING THE CROSSING PLACE OF **TWO WALKS** (1972) WHILE CROSSING DARTMOOR

DIARY ENTRIES

Day 3

Lady cooks breakfast at 7.30. Out into rain. Sharp hills. Over Bodmin Moor. Big views of both moors. Wind at back. TAMAR. Mushroom soup for lunch, tart and ice-cream. Up and down into Tavistock, rain squalls over Dartmoor. Into Two Bridges Hotel (phoned in from Horsebridge – the last single room…) Phone M. Salad, with great stride piano player. Wedding guests.

Day 9

Snowing at breakfast. Good scrambled eggs. Headwind over Downs. Swindon in sight. Raining and cold. Cut across over M-Way. Right fork to lunch pub. Best cheese and asparagus soup. Empty wet roads, under the Great Western Line by the Uffington Horse. Dry rest in church lobby. Less hedgerows. Headwinds. Nothing in first village. Past fantastic country house. Over swollen THAMES. Good flat road to Brampton. 2nd pub Yes! Phone M and Mum. Vietnamese landlady. Steak! Wash socks, turn up heater.

Day 12

V.G. breakfast with coach driver. Delicious brown bread and marmalade + croissant. Fast empty B-road, sunny and cold. Stop at Naseby Monument. Market Harborough, find open pub on high street, crisps and pudding, football on T.V. Fairly straight P.M., usual 4 P.M. blizzard from black cumulus clouds. Find open garage with shop, nice Indian owner, great ice-cream. On fast side road past viaduct in evening sun. First pub stop zilch, quick pint and on to next place. Snack meal in The Fox with cigar locals. Find good concealed camp 7.45 in dusk, behind hedge. Snow and rain in night.

Day 13

Watery dawn. Good sleep. Bounty. Into Melton Mowbray: 1. Bank 2. Paper 3. Breakfast, full monty by market. Out on small road north. Post back map No.2 from first village. Mixed skies. Dry tent at 12, stop on village green, ring Mum. Next village, Kit-Kat, Lilt, ring B from place with closed pub. On straight (down off high land now) to Granby. Look around for pub, very obscure, closed, but Irish lady opens up, makes a cheese sandwich. No more villages, keep going straight, 5 P.M. soft nap, past huge ex-quarry, into Newark 6.45. Find 'only' place, a town pub on main road. Big bath, wash socks. Fish and chips next door in empty dining room. V. hot hotel room. Longest mileage day.

Day 14

Relaxed breakfast on my own. Over Trent in rain. Heavy, and headwinds all day. Out to A1. Juggernauts and spray. Up bank too soon. Great wet stop at transport caff. On slip road at 10.15. 2 coffees, 45p. … Smaller roads, past power stations. Off to right, to nice-lady pub with coal fire at 1. Soup and sponge pud., 2 V.G. coffees and chat. On damp, chill P.M. Bit of main road near Gainsborough. Buy chocs at 6 and paper. No B&B, so fish and chips, 2 pots of tea, out in late sunshine – find great camp by canal – everything dry.

Day 23

2 coffees before breakfast, with radio 4. Down at 7.50, weetabix, prunes, grapefruit, poached egg in sunny corner. O.K. A-road. PEEBLES. Post and cards. On fast A.M., good going, sunny-ish. Rest on wall by Tweed. Write card to Tamsin. On to great mill pub at Blythe Bridge. Posh, easy chair by bar. Soup and profiteroles. On through lumpy drummlin country. Kit-Kat in garage shop. Buy food in poor-looking town. Orange juice. Out over Carstairs railway line. Huge black storm behind. Rain, and into miner's pub at Braehead for 3/4 hr. – "The Last Shift Inn". Out 6.30, still raining, theatrical skies. Find trees, camp on wet grass under rookery. Pork pie, picnic bar and apple, with drips from nests above.

Day 26

Lady a bit late for 7.30. Bran flakes. Gear up immediately in pouring rain with Dutch (?) cyclist in doorway. Straight, to Crieff. Buy map in info place. On 2 hours in pouring rain, first stop, an Inn. Coffee pot, with hot milk – 80p! On down, then up Sma 'Glen, over river, then up. Coffee rebounds…bit of diarrhoea behind rock. Next stop a tea room at junction with small road to glen. Great thick veg. soup and tea-cake. Chat to Eng. proprietor about walkers. Write post-card to Mum. On up glen in small showers (V.G. surface) past loch. Camera steamed-up from wet. Up very steep road over pass. Great views across top to Schiehallion and west. Rest on top in sun patch. Long down to loch, Kenmore Village. B&B just taken, so hotel – good value – best big bath with brown water. Ring Mum. Nice meal, comedy on T.V.

PORTUGUESE STONES

ONE STONE IN MONÇÃO

TWO STONES IN BRAGA

THREE STONES NEAR LIXA

FOUR STONES NEAR CINFÃES

FIVE STONES IN CARVALHOSA

SIX STONES NEAR VISEU

SEVEN STONES IN TONDELA

EIGHT STONES NEAR COIMBRA

NINE STONES IN BARQUEIRO

TEN STONES IN TOMAR

ELEVEN STONES NEAR ALPIARÇA

TWELVE STONES NEAR INFANTADO

THIRTEEN STONES IN MARATECA

FOURTEEN STONES IN ALCÁCER DO SAL

FIFTEEN STONES NEAR OURIQUE

SIXTEEN STONES NEAR VALE MARMELEIROS

SEVENTEEN STONES IN ALBUFEIRA

STONES PLACED BY THE ROADSIDE EACH DAY
ALONG A WALK OF 463 MILES
FROM THE NORTH TO THE SOUTH OF PORTUGAL

SPRING 2001

CLOUD MOUNTAIN STONES

A 15 DAY WALK IN THE THREE SISTERS WILDERNESS

OREGON 2001

Art as a formal and holistic description of the real space and experience of landscape and its most elemental materials.

Nature has always been recorded by artists, from pre-historic cave paintings to 20th century landscape photography. I too wanted to make nature the subject of my work, but in new ways. I started working outside using natural materials like grass and water, and this evolved into the idea of making a sculpture by walking.

Walking itself has a cultural history, from Pilgrims to the wandering Japanese poets, the English Romantics and contemporary long-distance walkers.

My first work made by walking, in 1967, was a straight line in a grass field, which was also my own path, going 'nowhere'. In the subsequent early map works, recording very simple but precise walks on Exmoor and Dartmoor, my intention was to make a new art which was also a new way of walking: walking as art. Each walk followed my own unique, formal route, for an original reason, which was different from other categories of walking, like travelling. Each walk, though not by definition conceptual, realised a particular idea. Thus walking – as art – provided an ideal means for me to explore relationships between time, distance, geography and measurement. These walks are recorded or described in my work in three ways: in maps, photographs or text works, using whichever form is the most appropriate for each different idea. All these forms feed the imagination, they are the distillation of experience.

Walking also enabled me to extend the boundaries of sculpture, which now had the potential to be de-constructed in the space and time of walking long distances. Sculpture could now be about place as well as material and form.

I consider my landscape sculptures inhabit the rich territory between two ideological positions, namely that of making 'monuments' or, conversely, of 'leaving only footprints'.

Over the years these sculptures have explored some of the variables of transience, permanence, visibility or recognition. A sculpture may be moved, dispersed, carried. Stones can be used as markers of time or distance, or exist as parts of a huge, yet anonymous, sculpture. On a mountain walk a sculpture could be made above the clouds, perhaps in a remote region, bringing an imaginative freedom about how, or where, art can be made in the world.

The press release for an exhibition at the Royal West of England Academy, Bristol 2000

Notes on Works 2000–2001

A TEXT is a description, or story, of a work in the landscape. It is the simplest and most elegant way to present a particular idea, which could be a walk, or a sculpture, or both.

Relationships are a fundamental theme of many works. I walk on a planet which circles the sun. Each day is a solar event. Time is measured in days, and walking time can be the measure of a country. WATER WALK also measures distance by rivers. A LINE OF 33 STONES A WALK OF 33 DAYS measures the days by stones. A CIRCLE OF MIDDAYS is a 12 day clockwise walk of 360 miles, being at a new point intersecting an imaginary circle at each midday. It is a text work which is an abstract map and clock. It is an emblematic distillation of walking time, and day-time, and of the degrees in a circle.

WALKING TO A SOLAR ECLIPSE is about time and place. It makes use of a cosmic event, the perfect alignment of Earth, Moon and Sun, as a unique moment which determines the destination of a walk. By contrast, in SINCHOLAGUA SUMMIT SHADOW STONES, the shadow of the volcano in Ecuador could pass across my stone circle after sunrise many times a year.

FROM UNCERTAINTY TO CERTAINTY: this work is a narrative of a dispersed sculpture which uses language, stones, chance, walking and Dartmoor.

In my sculptures, a stone is a stone, and I also use other raw materials like dust, water and mud, only to show their own innate natures. Similarly, I present objective time and space through the measurement of my walks.

Another level of reality, however, is the sub-atomic world, where particles are in a flux of changing relationships between speed, mass, positions and time. In AN EXCHANGE OF STONES AT A PLACE FOR A TIME ON DARTMOOR and THE SAME THING AT A DIFFERENT TIME AT A DIFFERENT PLACE, I wanted to make works that were metaphors for things that happen in particle physics. A walk is an event in space-time, and I may carry, scatter, concentrate or place stones, or exchange their places along a walk, as required. My stones are like sub-atomic particles in the space of the World. These works represent parallel phenomena at a different scale. Our human scale actually exists somewhere nearer the outer boundary of the universe than the sub-atomic limit.

SPEED OF THE SOUND OF LONELINESS is about relative speeds, with the metaphor changing from the micro to the cosmic scale. The title is taken from a song written by John Prine and sung by the country singer Nanci Griffith.

The world is continually in geological movement. Continental drift is at the speed our fingernails grow, and parts of Britain have come up from the South Atlantic. Nothing in the landscape is fixed; nothing has its 'eternal' place. Stones are always moving along in rivers and glaciers, being thrown out of volcanoes or clattering down mountains. Those works in which I move stones around are just another part of this continuum. The stones of A LINE OF 33 STONES A WALK OF 33 DAYS constitute an artwork, but of course are still autonomously and anonymously in the world, now as before. Yet they all also happen to be where they are now through the mediation of a moving common denominator, that is, me doing a walk. Each stone represents an interface of scales – one small stone represents a day in a walk of 1,030 miles. Each stone represents a kind of measurement of Britain, in relation to the speed of my walking and my route. Each stone has its geological history, yet perhaps momentarily, conceptually, symbolically or privately becomes 'something else' as well.

In WALKING STONES, by the action of a walk, stones get carried from day to day and from place to place. My work is another agent of change and placement. And walking is simple; stones are common and practical.

THROWING SNOW INTO A CIRCLE

A 7 DAY WALK IN THE GLÄRNISCH MASSIF

SWITZERLAND 1991

FOOTPATH WATERLINE
A 7 DAY WALK IN THE GLÄRNISCH MASSIF
SWITZERLAND 1991

SILBEREN STONES

NORTH AND SOUTH

A WALK OF 279 MILES

NORTHWARDS AND SOUTHWARDS

OUT AND BACK ON THE SAME ROAD

EIGHT WALKING HOURS EACH DAY

FIRST DAY	8 HOURS NORTH	FROM CHEPSTOW TO SADDLEBOW HILL
SECOND DAY	7 HOURS NORTH 1 HOUR SOUTH	FROM SADDLEBOW HILL TO NEAR LEOMINSTER
THIRD DAY	6 HOURS NORTH 2 HOURS SOUTH	FROM NEAR LEOMINSTER TO NEAR MIDDLETON
FOURTH DAY	5 HOURS NORTH 3 HOURS SOUTH	FROM NEAR MIDDLETON TO TUGFORD
FIFTH DAY	4 HOURS NORTH 4 HOURS SOUTH	FROM TUGFORD TO TUGFORD
SIXTH DAY	3 HOURS NORTH 5 HOURS SOUTH	FROM TUGFORD TO NEAR MIDDLETON
SEVENTH DAY	2 HOURS NORTH 6 HOURS SOUTH	FROM NEAR MIDDLETON TO NEAR LEOMINSTER
EIGHTH DAY	1 HOUR NORTH 7 HOURS SOUTH	FROM NEAR LEOMINSTER TO SADDLEBOW HILL
NINTH DAY	8 HOURS SOUTH	FROM SADDLEBOW HILL TO CHEPSTOW

WALES AND ENGLAND 1991

SCRAMBLING

ALONG THE COAST   THROUGH THE FOREST

NEAH BAY   BAHOBOHOSH POINT
SOOES BEACH   SHI SHI BEACH
POINT OF THE ARCHES   TSKAWAHYAH ISLAND
CAPE ALAVA   SAND POINT
YELLOW BANKS   KAYOSTLA BEACH
CEDAR CREEK   SOLEDUCK RIVER
FORKS   BOGACHIEL RIVER VALLEY
SOLEDUCK RIVER   DEER LAKE
APPLETON PASS   ELWHA RIVER   ELWHA

A FIVE DAY WALK ON THE OLYMPIC PENINSULA WASHINGTON 1991

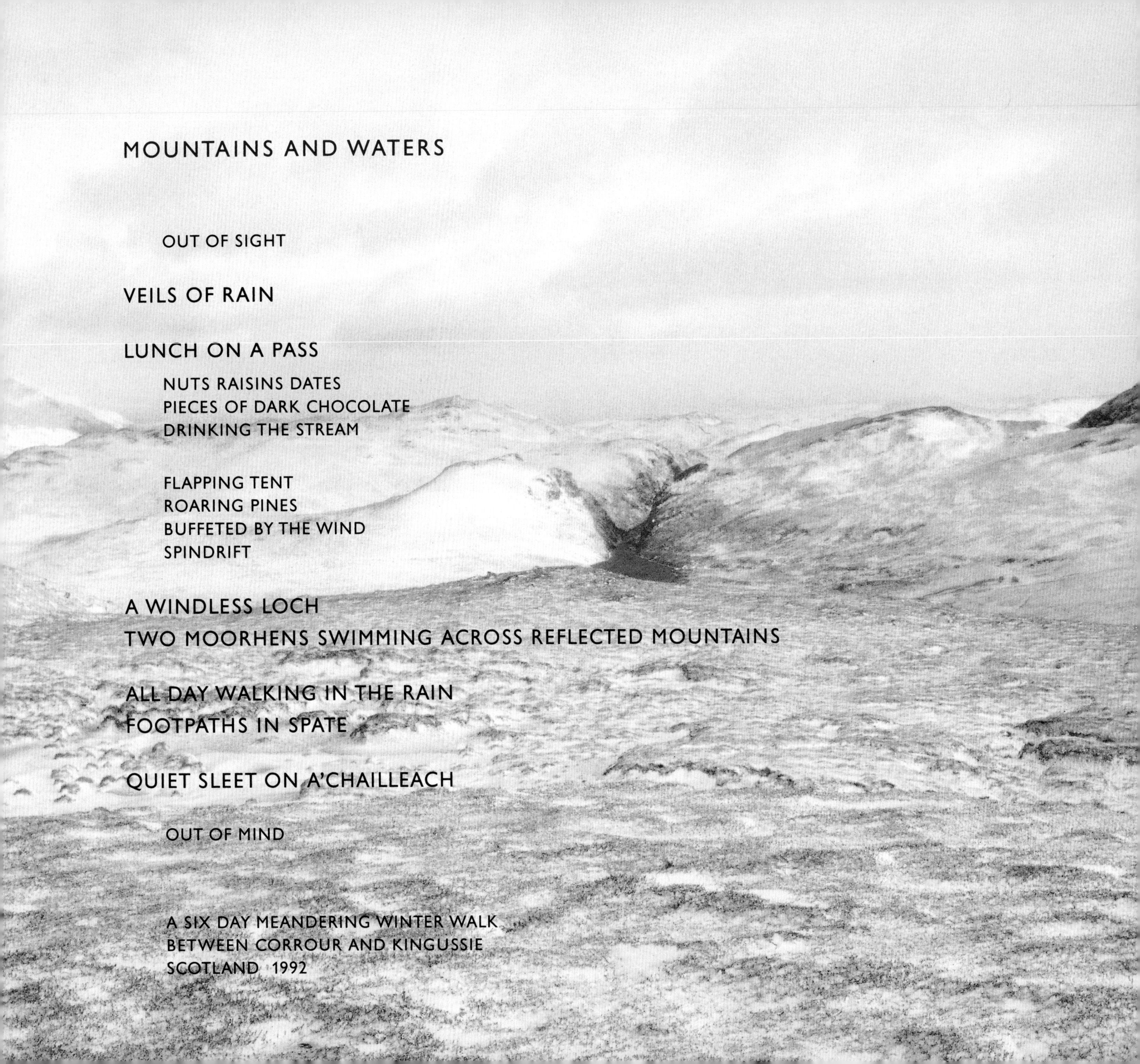

MOUNTAINS AND WATERS

OUT OF SIGHT

VEILS OF RAIN

LUNCH ON A PASS

    NUTS RAISINS DATES
    PIECES OF DARK CHOCOLATE
    DRINKING THE STREAM

    FLAPPING TENT
    ROARING PINES
    BUFFETED BY THE WIND
    SPINDRIFT

A WINDLESS LOCH
TWO MOORHENS SWIMMING ACROSS REFLECTED MOUNTAINS

ALL DAY WALKING IN THE RAIN
FOOTPATHS IN SPATE

QUIET SLEET ON A'CHAILLEACH

    OUT OF MIND

    A SIX DAY MEANDERING WINTER WALK
    BETWEEN CORROUR AND KINGUSSIE
    SCOTLAND 1992

MIND
ROCK

BEARING A ROCK IN MIND

AN ELEVEN DAY WALK IN THE MOUNTAINS NORTH OF KYOTO

BEGINNING AND ENDING
LOOKING AT THE SAME ROCK
AT RYOANJI

JAPAN WINTER 1992

ALONG THE WAY

FROM THE CAWING OF CROWS TO A SILVER-PAINTED STICK TO A GOLD BUDDHA
TO A GLASS OF SAKE A BOWL OF RICE AN ORANGE TO DEEP SNOW CAMP
TO A KINGFISHER TO GUSTS OF WARM AIR TO A CLEAR RIVER
TO A FULL STOMACH TO MIST ON SNOW TO THE SMILE OF AN OLD WOMAN
TO A WOODPECKER TO DRIPPING TREES PATTERING ON THE TENT TO LOGGING FIRES
TO A DIVING HAWK TO THE SMELL OF WOOD SAP TO BOAR SKINS DRYING IN THE SUN
TO SAWDUST TO A SLEEP IN THE SUN TO A HERON TO A CIRCLE FOR BASHŌ
TO A STOCKPILE OF NATURAL BOULDERS TO A MAN STRIPPING BARK TO THE CAWING OF CROWS

AN ELEVEN DAY WALK IN THE MOUNTAINS NORTH OF KYOTO JAPAN WINTER 1992

NOVEMBER SUNSHINE

A SEVEN DAY WALK OF 217 MILES IN DORSET

THE COMBINED TIME EACH DAY OF WALKING WITH MY SHADOW

FIRST DAY 1¾ HOURS

SECOND DAY 6¼ HOURS

THIRD DAY ½ HOUR

FOURTH DAY NO SUN

FIFTH DAY ¼ HOUR

SIXTH DAY 4 HOURS

SEVENTH DAY 3¼ HOURS

ENGLAND 1991

CROSSING THE DUZON
A ROAD WALK OF 586 MILES IN 18½ DAYS FROM BORDEAUX TO TURIN
1992

T I D E
W A L K

ENGLISH CHANNEL TO BRISTOL CHANNEL

A WALK OF TWO AND A HALF TIDES
RELATIVE TO THE WALKER

A CONTINUOUS WALK OF 104 MILES
FROM THE MORNING HIGH TIDE AT PLYMOUTH
TO THE AFTERNOON LOW TIDE AT WESTON-SUPER-MARE THE NEXT DAY

EBB AND FLOOD EBB AND FLOOD EBB

1992

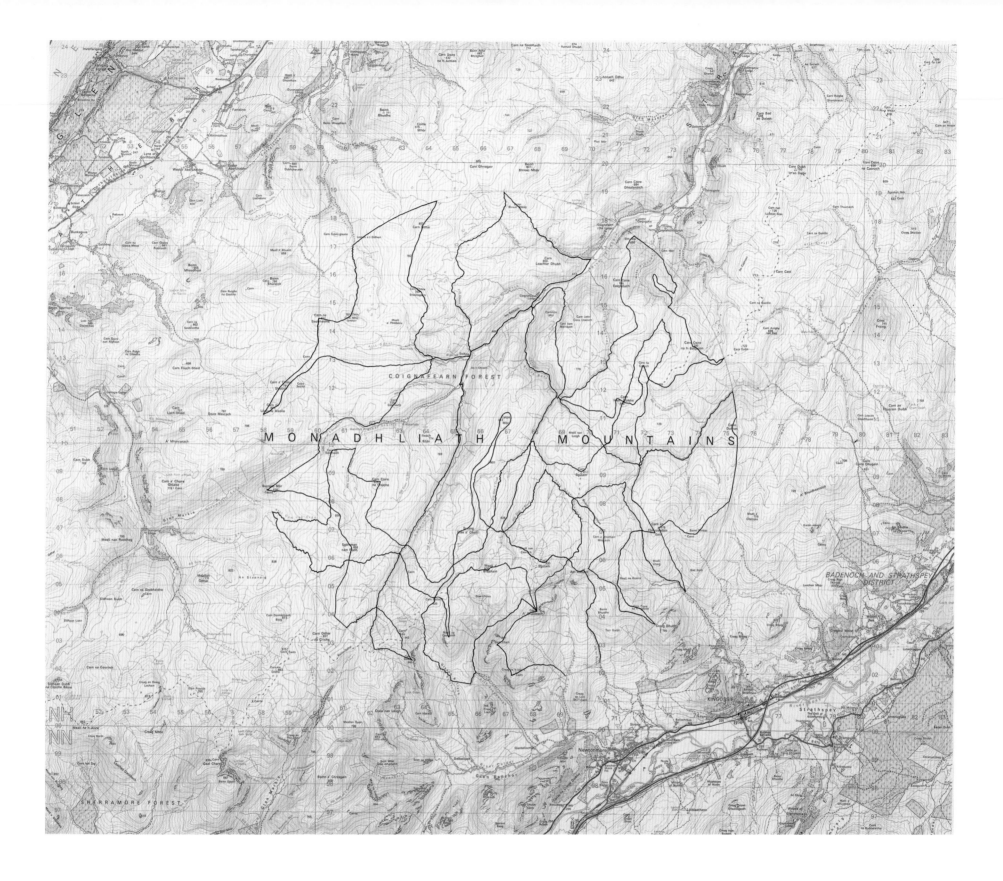

NO WHERE

A WALK OF 131 MILES WITHIN AN IMAGINARY CIRCLE

TEN DAYS AND NIGHTS

SCOTLAND 1993

NOTES ON MAPS 1994

A map can be used to make a walk. A map can be used to make a work of art.

Maps have layers of information; they show history, geography, the naming of places.

A map is an artistic and poetic combination of image and language.

For me, a map is a potent alternative to a photograph, it has a different function.

It can show the idea of a whole work, not a moment.

A map can show time and space in a work of art.

Distance, the days of walking, the campsites, the shape of the walking, can be shown in one concise but rich image.

In some of my works, I find the best places to realise particular ideas by first looking at a map.

A map can decide place and idea, either or both.

Maps can be read in many different ways, they are a standard and universal language.

I like to think my work on a map exists equally with all the other information on it.

On a long walk a map becomes a familiar, trusted object, something to look at endlessly, without boredom.

I can look at the planned future and the completed past.

A map is light.

A map could save my life.

DUSTY TO MUDDY TO WINDY

A WALK OF 191 MILES IN 5 DAYS FROM BRISTOL TO TRURO

SNOWDROPS FAMILIAR ROADS FROM AVON INTO SOMERSET THE WELSH HILLS IN VIEW OVER THE MENDIPS
EXMOOR IN VIEW THE SOMERSET LEVELS THE LIGHTS OF FISHERMEN : HIGH TIDE ON THE RIVER PARRETT BLACK SMOCK INN

43 MILES

WATCHING BUZZARDS ACROSS THE BLACK DOWN HILLS INTO DEVON FOLLOWED BY A DOG
CLATTERING HOOVES ON THE ROAD QUIET WEATHER A NEW MOON THREE TUNS INN

41 MILES

DARTMOOR IN VIEW CROSSING THE RIVER EXE HEDGEROW DAFFODILS DUSTY LANES
UP ONTO DARTMOOR PASSING BENNETT'S CROSS AT DUSK THE HOOT OF AN OWL TWO BRIDGES

36 MILES

BODMIN MOOR IN VIEW DOWN OFF DARTMOOR CROSSING THE RIVER TAMAR INTO CORNWALL
FIVE HOURS OF RAIN ACROSS BODMIN MOOR IN MIST ORION BETWEEN RACING CLOUDS THE BARLEY SHEAF

40 MILES

MUDDY LANES FOLLOWING A HERD OF COWS CHINA CLAY TIPS KISSING GATE
ATLANTIC HORIZON A FOLLOWING WIND THE ROAD FLOODED ADMIRAL BOSCAWEN

31 MILES

ENGLAND 1993

WET WEATHER WALKING

A SOUTHWARD WALK ACROSS SWITZERLAND
222 MILES IN 7 ½ DAYS BY ROADS AND FOOTPATHS
FROM BASEL TO DIRINELLA FROM BORDER TO BORDER
CROSSING OVER EIGHT PASSES ALONG THE WAY

1993

LIGHT SNOW IN THE NIGHT

BREAKING CAMP ON THE FIFTH MORNING
ALONG A 7 DAY WALK OF 96 MILES
SOUTHWARDS ALONG THE SHENANDOAH MOUNTAINS

VIRGINIA SPRING 1993

OLD YEAR NEW YEAR WALK

THE LAST TWELVE HOURS OF 1992 – THE FIRST TWELVE HOURS OF 1993

A WALK OF 80 MILES IN 24 HOURS

MIDNIGHT NEAR NYTHE ON KING'S SEDGE MOOR SOMERSET ENGLAND

FIVE WALKS

A WALK OF 30 MILES

A WALK PASSING 30 FARMHOUSES (24 MILES)

A WALK CROSSING 30 CROSSROADS (34 MILES)

A WALK SEEING 30 BLACKBIRDS (29 MILES)

A WALK LASTING 30 HOURS (96 MILES)

SIX DAYS AND ONE NIGHT ENGLAND 1993

END

URINATING PLACES LINE

A CONTINUOUS WALK OF 96 MILES IN 30 HOURS FROM DAWLISH TO BRISTOL

SUNLIT WINDLESS STARLIT

ENGLAND 1993

START

A SOUTHWARD WALK OF 220 MILES IN 14 DAYS ACROSS THE MIDDLE OF ICELAND 1994

WIND CIRCLE

RAVEN CIRCLE

CIRCLE OF AUTUMN WINDS

READING THE WIND READING THE COMPASS

A WALK OF 46 MILES INSIDE AN IMAGINARY CIRCLE ON DARTMOOR
ENGLAND 1994

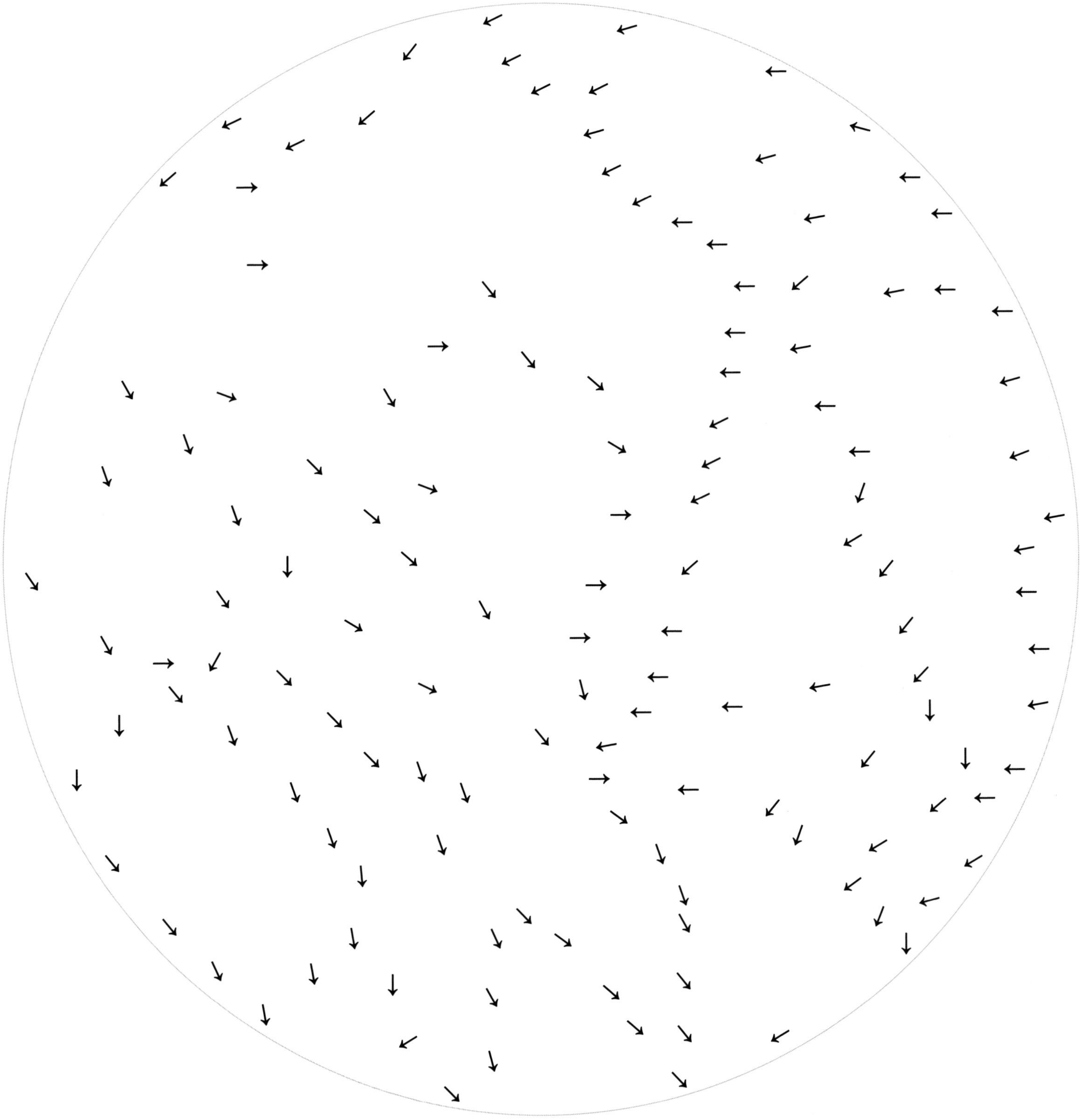

ASH LINE
EIGHT DAYS WALKING IN CENTRAL QUEENSLAND
AUSTRALIA 1994

MIDSUMMER DAY'S WALK

ON GLASTONBURY TOR AT NOON

A WALK OF 59 MILES BETWEEN SUNRISE AND SUNSET

ENGLAND 1994

FOUR DAYS AND FOUR CIRCLES

A FOUR DAY WALK ON DARTMOOR FROM SOUTH TO NORTH

WALKING FOR EIGHT HOURS EACH DAY IN EACH CIRCLE

ENGLAND 1994

LEAVING THE STONES
A FIVE DAY WALK WITH DOGS ON SPITZBERGEN
SVALBARD NORWAY 1995

DARTMOOR TIME

A CONTINUOUS WALK OF 24 HOURS ON DARTMOOR

$1^1/_2$ HOURS OF EARLY MORNING MIST

THE SPLIT SECOND CHIRRUP OF A SKYLARK

SKIRTING THE BRONZE AGE GRIMSPOUND

FORDING THE WEST DART RIVER IN TWO MINUTES

PASSING A PILE OF STONES PLACED SIXTEEN YEARS AGO

A CROW PERCHED ON GREAT GNATS' HEAD CAIRN FOR FIVE MINUTES

HOLDING A BUTTERFLY WITH A LIFESPAN OF ONE MONTH

CLIMBING OVER GRANITE 350 MILLION YEARS OLD ON GREAT MIS TOR

THINKING OF A FUTURE WALK

EIGHT HOURS OF MOONLIGHT

55 MILES

ENGLAND AUTUMN 1995

EVOLUTION CIRCLE

A WALK OF 12 DAYS IN THE HIGH SIERRA

CALIFORNIA 1995

MUIR PASS STONES

EVENING CAMP STONES

DUSTLINES

KICKING UP A LINE OF DUST EACH DAY ALONG THE WALKING LINE

A 7 DAY WALK ON THE EAST BANK OF THE RIO GRANDE

EL CAMINO REAL NEW MEXICO 1995

THE GIANT'S CAUSEWAY

MINCE BEEF AND ONION PIES

RATHER YOU THAN ME

DRIZZLE

FIRST BIRD OF PREY

FAST CLOUDS

LAMBS

WASHING BAY

A WRONG FORK

POTATOES BLUES FOR SALE

SHARING A POT OF TEA AT A GARAGE

A REST IN A STRAW BARN

A WRONG FORK

IT'S A BEAUTIFUL MILD MORNING

DRIZZLE

B. D. FLOOD LTD OLDCASTLE

SUPPER IN A KITCHEN BEING DECORATED

POTATOES PINKS FOR SALE

MAHON'S COSY SNUG

THE ROAD FLOODED

A COFFEE IN A FLOODED BAR THE SLIEVE BLOOM

THE ROAD FLOODED

OPEN TRENCHES AHEAD

WAITING WITH LOCALS FOR A MIDDAY OPENING

IT'S GOING TO BE BAD ALL DAY AND TOMORROW

WELCOME TO TIPPERARY TOWN

THE BALLYHOURA WAY

IT'S FROSTY THIS MORNING

POTHOLED ROAD

WRINGING OUT SOCKS IN A CHURCH

LONG'S BAR AND LOUNGE MALLOW

A CAMP IN THE BOGGERAGH MOUNTAINS

RAINBOW

THE ROAD FLOODED

FRIDAY MOUNTAIN BOG MEN

THE ROAD FLOODED

FOLLOWED BY A DOG FOR FIVE MILES

THE AHACRINDUFF RIVER IN SPATE

PLEASE LOOK FOR A LOOSE HORSE

A WRONG TURN

BALTIMORE BEACON

ALL IRELAND WALK

A WALK OF 382 MILES IN 12 DAYS FROM THE SOUTH COAST TO THE NORTH COAST OF IRELAND

WINTER 1995

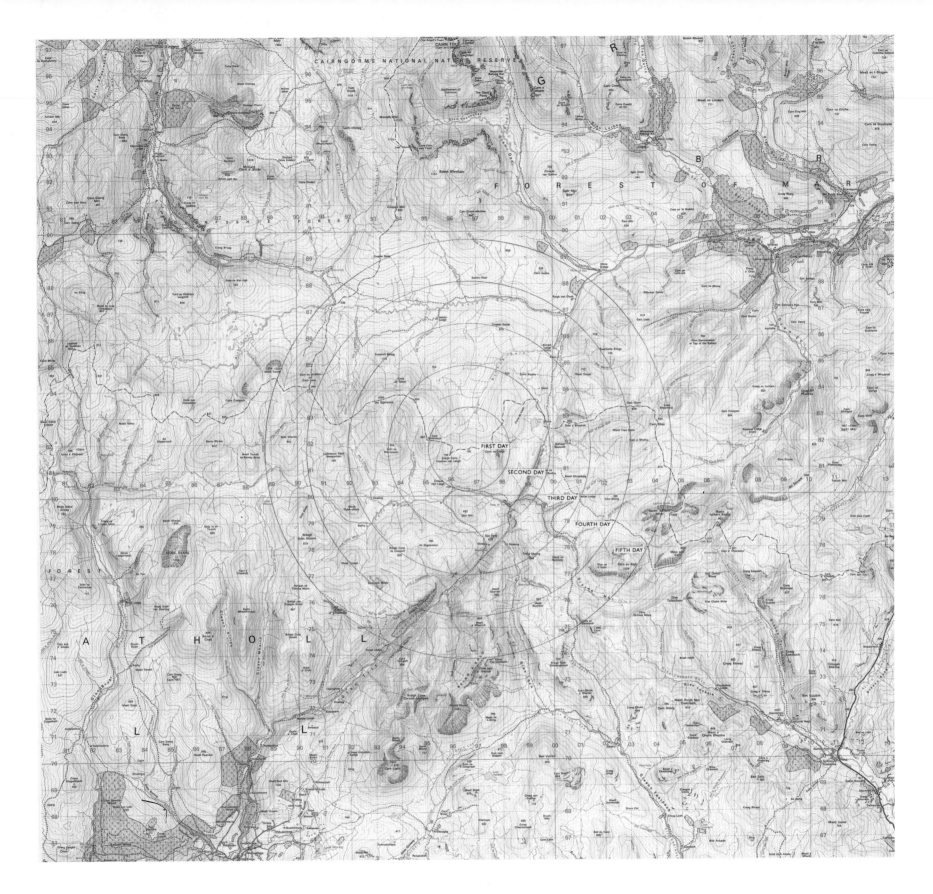

FIRST DAY

SECOND DAY

THIRD DAY

FOURTH DAY

FIFTH DAY

CONCENTRIC DAYS

EACH DAY A MEANDERING WALK SOMEWHERE WITHIN AND TO THE EDGE OF EACH CIRCLE

SCOTLAND 1996

MONGOLIA 1996

ASIA CIRCLE STONES

MONGOLIA 1996

HERD DROPPINGS

NOMAD CIRCLE

WALKING TO A LUNAR ECLIPSE

FROM A MIDDAY HIGH TIDE AT AVONMOUTH
A WALK OF 366 MILES IN 8 DAYS
ENDING AT A MIDNIGHT TOTAL ECLIPSE OF THE FULL MOON

A LEAP YEAR WALK ENGLAND 1996

HOURS
MILES

A WALK OF 24 HOURS : 82 MILES

A WALK OF 24 MILES IN 82 HOURS

ENGLAND 1996

A WALK IN A GREEN FOREST

TWO SNAKES   A DOUBLE HALO AROUND THE SUN   CROAKING FROGS
SUMMER AIR CONDENSING OVER WINTER SNOW   RAIN HAMMERING ON THE TENT
RIVERS TURNING FROM CLEAR TO MUDDY   CLOUDY NIGHT NO-MOON BLACKNESS
A MUD SLIDE   ROCKS CRACKING TO THE TOUCH   GLOW-WORMS
WATCHING MOONLIGHT TURNING INTO DAWN   THE FOOTPATH PASSING THROUGH A CLEFT TREE
A NIGHT OF THUNDER AND LIGHTNING   A LARGE CHESTNUT TREE STRUCK DOWN
A FAMILY OF MONKEYS   THE MILKY WAY SHINING BETWEEN THE CRESTS OF A RAVINE
MAGNOLIA TREES LIKE PATCHES OF SNOW   CUCKOOS AND WOODPECKERS
SITTING ON A MOUNTAINTOP AMID BEECHES AND BAMBOO   THE DAYTIME RACKET OF FOREST LIFE
SLEEPING BY THE SOUNDS OF A RIVER AND A WATERFALL   UNDER A TREE THE CHAOTIC BEAT OF RAINDROPS
STREAMS RISING AND FALLING WITH PASSING DOWNPOURS   BREAKING CAMP AND BREAKING A CIRCLE
A WINDLESS WALK   TADPOLES AND LILAC

EIGHT DAYS WALKING IN THE SHIRAKAMI MOUNTAINS

AOMORI JAPAN 1997

EARLY SUMMER CIRCLE

AOMORI 1997

SHIRAKAMI LINE

AOMORI 1997

CAMP STONES
AOMORI 1997

A CIRCLE OF MIDDAYS

WALKING 360 MILES AROUND A CIRCLE

A CLOCKWISE AND MEANDERING WALK OF 12 DAYS
INTERSECTING EACH DAY AT MIDDAY
WITH AN IMAGINARY CIRCLE 63 MILES WIDE

GLOUCESTERSHIRE WILTSHIRE HAMPSHIRE DORSET DEVON SOMERSET

ENGLAND 1997

MIDDAY MIDDAY MIDDAY MIDDAY

MIDDAY MIDDAY

MIDDAY MIDDAY

MIDDAY MIDDAY

MIDDAY MIDDAY

PATAGONIA 1997

TIERRA DEL FUEGO CIRCLE

ALONG A SIX DAY WINTER WALK

ARGENTINA 1997

TO BUILD A FIRE

A SIX DAY WINTER WALK ON TIERRA DEL FUEGO
BUILDING A FIRE EACH DAY AT EACH CAMPSITE ALONG THE WAY

ASHES BLOWING IN THE WIND

ARGENTINA 1997

WALKING A CIRCLE BY THE BEAGLE CHANNEL

TIERRA DEL FUEGO ARGENTINA 1997

FROM LINE TO LINE

A BOOT-HEEL LINE IN DUST IN RIO MAYO

A BOOT-HEEL LINE IN DUST IN PERITO MORENO

A BOOT-HEEL LINE IN MUD IN CALETA OLIVIA

A BOOT-HEEL LINE IN MUD IN FITZ ROY

A BOOT-HEEL LINE IN MUD IN PUERTO SAN JULIÁN

A BOOT-HEEL LINE IN SNOW IN RIO GALLEGOS

A BOOT-HEEL LINE ON ICE IN ESPERANZA

A BOOT-HEEL LINE IN DUST IN EL CALAFATE

A BOOT-HEEL LINE IN SNOW IN TOLHUIN

A BOOT-HEEL LINE IN SNOW IN USHUAIA

PATAGONIA AND TIERRA DEL FUEGO

ARGENTINA 1997

A SICILIAN WALK

A SOUTHWARD WALK ACROSS SICILY OF 111 MILES IN 3 DAYS FROM PALERMO TO AGRIGENTO

FILLING MY WATER BOTTLE FROM A CEMETARY TAP NEAR PIANA DEGLI ALBANESI

ASKING THE WAY FROM A FARMER PLOUGHING

GROUPS OF MEN TALKING AND SMOKING IN CORLEONE TOWN SQUARE

A HELICOPTER BY THE ROADSIDE NEAR PRIZZI

THROWING STONES AT A PACK OF DOGS NEAR BIVONA

CIANCIANA THRONGED WITH TEENAGERS IN THE EVENING

WALKING A STRAIGHT EMPTY ROAD IN LINE UNDER THE MILKY WAY

STOPPING AT MIDNIGHT FOR A SLEEP IN LONG GRASSES BY THE PLATANI RIVER

WALKING OVER A PASS FROM DARKNESS TO FIRST LIGHT TO SUNRISE

A VIEW OF A GREEK TEMPLE IN THE HOT SUN

ITALY 1997

UP AND DOWN

ONE SUMMIT LEADS TO ANOTHER

FROM LECKAVREA MOUNTAIN 2174 FT.

TO LETTERBRECKAUN 2193 FT.

TO BENBAUN 2395 FT.

TO BENCOLLAGHDUFF 2290 FT.

TO BENCORR 2336 FT.

TO DERRYCLARE 2220 FT.

TO BENBREEN 2276 FT.

TO BENGOWER 2184 FT.

TO BENLETTERY 1904 FT.

TO BENGLENISKY 1710 FT.

TO BENCULLAGH 2073 FT.

TO MUCKANAGHT 2153 FT.

TO BENFREE 2093 FT.

TO BENBRACK 1922 FT.

TO DOUGHRUAGH 1725 FT.

TO ALTNAGAIGHERA 1781 FT.

TO GARRAUN 1973 FT.

TO BENCHOONA 1919 FT.

TO DEVILSMOTHER 2131 FT.

TO BEN GORM 2303 FT.

TO MWEELREA 2688 FT.

TO OUGHTY CRAGGY 2610 FT.

A SEVEN DAY WALK IN THE MOUNTAINS OF CONNEMARA AND SOUTH MAYO

IRELAND EARLY SPRING 1997

STONES ON OUGHTY CRAGGY
ALONG A SEVEN DAY WALK IN CONNEMARA AND SOUTH MAYO
IRELAND EARLY SPRING 1997

ECUADOR 1998

SIXTH MORNING CAMP

BONES

HERE AND THERE BLEACHED BONES SCATTERED ON THE PÁRAMO

HERE AND THERE THE LONG BONES PLACED IN LINE FOLLOWING THE WALKING LINE

ALONG THE TREK DE CÓNDOR ON A 12 DAY WALK IN ECUADOR 1998

COTOPAXI CIRCLE

SUNRISE CIRCLE

SUNRISE AT 19,346 FEET

A CIRCLE DRAWN IN THE SNOW ON THE SUMMIT OF VOLCÁN COTOPAXI

ALONG A WALK OF 12 DAYS IN ECUADOR 1998

DIARY ENTRIES

Day 2

Dew. Up 5.45. Away 7 up zig-zag south from lake. Through cloud forest, a muddy trail. Rest with midges. Cross river, drink, up to big views. Trail petered out, so very tiring. 11.30 drink/pill, lunch at water-hole. Pick up better trail, up and over to lake. Nice track. Small recce. up over into next valley, small lake. Walk downstream. Perfect short grass by stream. Wash feet. Hail shower, windier. Plan route map in tent.

Day 3

Wet tent. Relaxed breakfast. On down to track – back up towards Antisana. Over brow and contour along ridge. See good camp-site – water, shelter, on edge of amphitheatre. Pitch. Pack day stuff, up to ridge and around. Big fast birds. Views of clouding Antisana. Lunch rest at 11.30 (water a bit brackish). Bomb up peak – Antisanilla. Snooze in hot sun at top, surrounded by changing clouds. Leisurely P.M. down. Get water from lake, firewood. Tea. Feel acclimatized (headache gone). The loud buzzings are humming birds.

Day 4

Perfect breakfast fire with views of Cotopaxi and Sincholagua. Night clouds gone. On down good going, bleached bones, wide plain. Over hillock, a grey sand area, good stop at river. Drink. Follow track up, strong going. Rest. Over small pass, drop down to 'pond' with floating grass, for lunch. Contour down around wide valley, over and down to river with 'works'. Rest. Over to next river, recce. up to find place out of wind. Backtrack to good place. Wash feet. Tea (weak gaz). Dandelions flush to the ground, blue flowers, russet "cacti", bright green moss hummocks. Second boy with gun, at 6… Flashes of lightning at night in the east from the 'Oriente', intimations of the Amazonas.

Day 5

Good sleep. Warm gaz in sleeping bag. <u>Very</u> heavy dew, frozen. Try and wait for sun on tent to melt the frost. Over ridge and up the shoulder. Decide to keep to the ridge, on left side of big valley. Find water on top! Fantastic 360 views of horizons. Keep going over ridge hills. Rest on bluff. Swooping birds of prey. See water, campsite, etc. Down to lunch, fresh water. Snooze on moss. On to great camp-site, crystal cool water. Leave rucksac, up and along ridge. Stay one hour, facing Antisana. Great cloud day. Down to pitch tent in P.M. sun. Dry socks. Sheltered, mossy place. Tea.

Day 6

Sun on tent. Bit hazy. Warm gaz in bag. Photos during b-fast. Up over pass, around, stop at shoulder. Up to ridge hill, views of Cotopaxi, small circle. On down right into gully. Dry tent. Stop for drink at first water and trees. Good path down. Branch right to river below ridge. Rest. On to lunch for 1 hr. Then up ridge with rucksac, ½ hr to top, zig-zagging. Recce. for water. Find 2 drips. Leave bottle and collect rucksac. ¾ hr. Carefully positioning both bottles. Rig waterproof for wind-break. Find OK camp, bit sheltered, firewood. Tired. Cloudy, bit windy. <u>Very comfy camp</u>.

Day 10

Naturally, think I didn't sleep, even being so quiet, moonlight through the window. So much to anticipate. People stirring at 12.45 A.M. Get up, make tea in kitchen, everyone going around by torchlight, except Alfredo!… Give 'A' a shout at 1.30. Finally he comes down and starts making a huge meal – more patties, guacamole, rice pudding, me getting so full and just wanting to be off. 'A' endlessly sorted his chaotic gear, finally stowed my rucksac in 'security' cupboard – no lock – away about 2.30, <u>way</u> after the others. Decided to wear my down jacket, also fitted up with harness. 10 mins. to glacier then on with the crampons – very nervous but concentrated. No fluffs. Then – to it! Up first pitch in windless moonlight, broken cloud. Soon roped up, belayed over some crevasses. Soon see lights ahead and pass 'early' party. Get stuck then accelerate to overtake. Only the change of pace tiring. Bit of a headache. Everything magical. Feel O.K. except for <u>full</u> stomach nerves) and head. Take 2 paracetemols with water from A's flask. We keep up a fast pace – the big rock band soon in view and passed. Through a big crevasse. Some steep pitches, one very exposed, belayed with ice-stake. Get the hang of the rope and team-work very well. Naturally towards the top some huge steep curves. Suddenly patch of light in sky, moonlight rapidly fades to dawn. Great adrenalin energy near top, a final surge to the beautiful domed summit. Photo of A in the sunrise. Great crater. Magical first half-hour of all the light changing on mountains on all horizons. Clear, still, magical conditions. A unfolds a small special bag and places a sacred, exotic, mixed-rock circle in the snow, reads from an old dilapidated book in front of it. Beautiful. We have a great hour-in-the-life, talk. Finally we head down, me in front now, no nerves, calm, stunning mixed views of distant brown plains, snow and ice. Put on glasses and cream. Pass the others, coming up slow and gasping, at the dangerous snow-stake pitch. Great descent, finally off with crampons, back to Refuge at 8.30-ish. Tired but exalted. Rest on bed, make tea for us both. No-one else in Refuge, a quiet time. A makes good potato-garlic-onion soup (salty). <u>Coffee</u>. Re-pack sack. A needs some transport money, so give him a 100 bill and get some change – useful, so I won't need a bank in Quito. Away at 11. Give A my gaz burner and cylinders, he gives me his 'bread' and cheese. Very dusty and soft trail. Half way down – a sudden hail storm. Dust cloud puffs on the dirt road. But it doesn't pass over, it goes on and on – the landscape gets white and I get wet and stoned. A few day-tripping Indian families in pick-ups. Finally a thunder storm gets locked between the two mountains, so I cross the plain in pouring rain and thunder. Head across to the lake camp-site. Pitch in light rain, 1.30, firewood out of the question. Sleeping bag O.K. Rains all afternoon. Nuts, try the uncooked bread and cheese. Yum. Un-typical weather in this semi-desert, dusty landscape, but … clears up just in time to make great camp-fire… with 'manioc' bread. Trousers drying on tree, shirt drying in the wood smoke.

(Alfredo was a Venezuelan Indian guide I met on Cotopaxi by chance)

As well as making art only by walking, walking also is a way to find the beautiful landscapes of the planet. One of the forms that my work takes is to make sculptures along the way.

My work takes many forms, but what you will see today is mainly the photographs of the sculptures and the landscapes.

There is a Chinese saying that says that every long journey starts with the first footstep. This is literally the start of the footpath that leads to Everest. Walking to Everest is not a continuous trail. It's really more like walking from one village to the next village, and if you join all the trails up, you come to Everest. This is looking at Everest from the highest point of a twenty-one day walk. In the foreground is the Kumbu Glacier which comes down from the icefall. So the next day I made this line on the glacier. It is never my intention to make permanent or monumental works in the landscape. I liked the idea that this line would break up and disappear as the glacier moved down the valley.

This is a line in Scotland. If I think the place is really beautiful, I will replace all the stones before I leave. These are very large stones, so I have not moved them, I have just made them upright. So it was easy to place them back in their original positions.

This is a line made by walking up and down many times. It was made on a seven-day wandering walk in Lapland. So on a long walk I made a sculpture just by walking in a different way, so the walking becomes a ritual. Walking within walking.

A lot of my work is leaving traces which share the same place as other traces of animals. As well as my line, if you look closely, you can see the tracks of the animals. I think that the surface of the world anywhere is a record of all its human, animal and geographical history.

The lines I've shown you up to now, I've made with my hands, but this was made with my feet by kicking the stones together. It seems appropriate that on a long walk in Bolivia, on foot, I can also make sculptures with my feet. Usually the work is made in whichever way is the easiest or most appropriate.

This is a very early work from Arizona in 1971. Made by dragging my boot-heel.

This is back on the west coast of Ireland. Usually I don't go back to visit my sculptures, but by chance I took this photograph fifteen years after I had made the work.

I don't know why, but this is one of my favourite works, from Scotland. I think you'll notice that because I use mostly lines and circles, the artistic decisions in my work are choosing the places, not choosing the forms.

Sometimes if I'm climbing a high mountain, it's a good idea to spend one day half way up to get acclimatised. I find quite often that I make my sculptures on rest days like this or at stopping places, because it's when I rest or stop that I can sit down and look at the landscape in a more relaxed way. In other words, it's only when I'm resting I have more time to think about art.

This is my home landscape quite near where I live in England. The pile of stones is one of my works. It is 1,449 stones placed at 1,449 feet above sea level. So in one way it is an anonymous pile of stones, but in another way it is about the idea of relating the stones and this place, to the sea level. I like the idea that a lot of my works can be unrecognisable as art unless you know the story of their meaning.

One of the pleasures of walking is the pleasure of finding a nice campsite. Finding a good campsite is a daily ritual. It could be finding a good place out of the wind or near fresh water or near firewood. In this work I've combined the pleasures of putting up my tent and making a sculpture.

The only way to make a walk in the Sierra Madre Mountains in Mexico is to follow the rivers in the canyons. Every day we were crossing in and out of the rivers and drying our boots and socks, and the stick is for helping to cross the rivers, also. Because the river was the key to being there, for drinking water, and also being the way through the mountains, it seemed appropriate to make my art also from water. All the art I made on that particular walk was just by pouring water marks from my water bottle, onto the hot dry boulders.

I'm going to show you just a few slides of places along the way. In the Himalayas, the way to be in the mountains is by following the footpaths from village to village, and I liked the idea that they're communal ways, and everyone is walking on the footpath for their own different reasons. I'm walking to make art, and that lady is walking to carry firewood. One of the works I made on that trip was to literally brush the path clean of leaves.

Of course on these walks there are many places where you see interesting things or other art. And this is a famous Menai wall. This is a communal object where each monk would carve a prayer on a stone and add the stone to the wall. Art and reality.

I am sometimes asked why there are no people in the photographs I take of my work. Of course in the mountains, people are very important, for showing the way, hospitality, getting food. But it's just that people are not the subject of my work. My work is about lines and stones and walking. It's really just a choice. My art is about my work, and the social life is just separate. I mean, all art is about a choice from the endless possibilities of life, but in fact each artist does have to make a choice and find his or her language.

These are the Hoggar Mountains in the center of the Sahara Desert. I was really lucky on this walk, because it rained for the first time in five years just before I arrived, so there were small pools of water in the mountains. I was able to walk from pool to pool, and each day the pools got smaller and smaller, until the sixth day when they had all dried up, so that was the end of the walk. For me that was a kind of beautiful and poetic logic.

I like to think that when I make images, that it is not just a circle, it is really the centrepoint of the whole place, right from the circle to the horizon. Because naturally each place exists as far as the eye can see.

These last two works, as well as the sculpture themselves, are also about alignments. It's about the alignment of the viewer, to the work, to the horizon. A lot of my work is about the relationships of the position of the observer to the landscape, like being on the mountaintop, between the sun, and the sunrise shadow.

This is a campsite from a walk in France. With a snail drawing on the tent. I started this walk with the idea to walk across France, but I noticed that it was completely blue skies each day, so I decided to finish the walk when I saw the first cloud. So it was called *A Cloudless Walk*. A three-and-a-half-day walk from the mouth of the Loire to the first cloud. The walk started at a very solid geographic place, and ended, by chance, with an ephemeral phenomenon like a cloud. One of the things I like about walking is that just the simple and very normal act of days of walking can carry quite interesting ideas.

This is a typical view of an English country lane on a walk from the west coast to the east coast of England. Each day I carried a different stone in my pocket. From stone to stone, from day to day. So the work was called *Walking Stones* and it was eleven days and eleven stones.

This was from a very interesting show in Paris called 'Magicians of the Earth', which was the first completely international show of contemporary art from all over the world. You could really see that we live in a world of parallel cultures.

This is my *Red Mud Circle*, with a ground drawing by Australian Aborigines.

You might have realized that, as well as stones, water is a very important theme and idea in my work. If I make a water drawing in the landscape, I use just water and take a photograph of the image. But to do a similar thing in a gallery, it's much better to mix the water with mud thrown on the walls. And by the way, it's the same River Avon mud that I used in the gallery here. I use my local mud, because it's beautiful … where I was born, it's the river that has the second highest tide in the world.

This is a small gallery show in Italy, and this is to show you how I sometimes use mud with my hands on the floor. Walls and floor, it's all the same to me.

This is the Guggenheim Museum in New York. As well as the sculpture, you can see on the wall behind, my text works and photo works in the frames. When I have an exhibition, the real sculpture feeds the senses directly, and the photographs and the texts feed the imagination.

My work is a balance between the reality of seeing real stones, and then a photograph of perhaps a stone circle made many thousands of miles away. And that idea is a freedom both for me, as the artist making the work, and also, I hope, for the viewer.

Another thing I like about my mud is that it's very practical. I can travel around the world with just a small handful and make a large work when I arrive.

Of course, in the Guggenheim Museum, all my straight lines became arcs. So I like to think of my work as quite adaptable and flexible.

Like the mud work I've made here in the museum, this is a very watery mud work done in a very fast way to make splashes.

Three works from a museum in Sydney. Again this is to show two mud works of different character. So one aspect of the mud works is that the top line is made by my hands, and all the splashes are made by nature. So, in a way, what I do shows you the natural force of gravity and water. So I only have to make some of the work, and nature does the rest.

This is a small stone sculpture from my home in Bristol.

Just to end, I'm going to read these words about my work:

REALITY

TIME

MEMORY

SLEEPING

COUNTING

LANGUAGE

BOOTS

SOLITUDE

MAPS

MUSIC

TENT

HUMOUR

DISTANCE

INTUITION

EXPERIENCE

CHANCE

LOVE

SPEED OF THE SOUND OF LONELINESS

(IF CROW TOR REPRESENTS THE SUN)

A CONTINUOUS WALK ON DARTMOOR BETWEEN SUNRISE AND SUNSET

WALKING A CIRCULAR PATH AROUND CROW TOR
CORRESPONDING TO THE DISTANCE OF THE EARTH IN ITS ORBIT AROUND THE SUN
A CIRCLE 7 MILES IN CIRCUMFERENCE WALKED $3^{1}/_{2}$ TIMES

MY WALKING SPEED 2.8 MILES AN HOUR

(THE ROTATION SPEED OF THE EARTH IN ENGLAND 700 MILES AN HOUR)
(THE ROTATION SPEED OF THE EARTH IN ITS ORBIT AROUND THE SUN 70,000 MILES AN HOUR)
(THE SPEED OF OUR MOTION AROUND THE GALAXY 500,000 MILES AN HOUR)

WINTER 1998

WALKS OF CHANCE

WALKS CARRYING A BAG OF ELEVEN PEBBLES WITH A WORD WRITTEN ON EACH

UP DOWN END FAST SLOW NORTH SOUTH EAST WEST STRAIGHT MEANDERING

EACH WALK IS REALISED BY OBSERVING THIS SYSTEM:
THE PEBBLES ARE DRAWN AT RANDOM OUT OF THE BAG ONE BY ONE AT INDETERMINATE INTERVALS
EACH PEBBLE IS RETURNED TO THE BAG WHILE THE WALK PROCEEDS BY FOLLOWING THE WORD ON THAT PEBBLE
THIS PROCEDURE IS REPEATED FROM PEBBLE TO PEBBLE UNTIL THE END PEBBLE IS DRAWN

EAST FAST UP SOUTH UP STRAIGHT SOUTH MEANDERING NORTH WEST NORTH UP FAST END

EAST UP END

UP SLOW STRAIGHT STRAIGHT MEANDERING SOUTH FAST END

FAST STRAIGHT SOUTH DOWN SLOW SOUTH STRAIGHT STRAIGHT NORTH EAST DOWN WEST SOUTH END

DOWN WEST MEANDERING UP STRAIGHT MEANDERING SLOW FAST DOWN SOUTH DOWN SLOW END

FAST MEANDERING UP SLOW NORTH END

DARTMOOR ENGLAND 1998

FROM UNCERTAINTY TO CERTAINTY

FROM TEN PEBBLES TO NO PEBBLES

A WALK CARRYING A BAG OF PEBBLES WITH A WORD WRITTEN ON EACH

UP DOWN FAST SLOW NORTH SOUTH EAST WEST STRAIGHT MEANDERING

THE PEBBLES ARE DRAWN AT RANDOM OUT OF THE BAG
ONE BY ONE AT INDETERMINATE INTERVALS. EACH IS PLACED
ON THE GROUND AND THE WALK PROCEEDS FROM THAT PLACE
BY FOLLOWING THE WORD ON THE PEBBLE. THIS PROCEDURE
IS REPEATED FROM PEBBLE TO PEBBLE UNTIL THE BAG IS EMPTY.

FIRST PEBBLE WALKING EAST

SECOND PEBBLE WALKING STRAIGHT

THIRD PEBBLE SLOW WALKING

FOURTH PEBBLE WALKING DOWN

FIFTH PEBBLE WALKING FAST

SIXTH PEBBLE WALKING WEST

SEVENTH PEBBLE WALKING NORTH

EIGHTH PEBBLE MEANDERING WALKING

NINTH PEBBLE WALKING SOUTH

TENTH PEBBLE WALKING UP

DARTMOOR ENGLAND 1998

A WALK ACROSS IRELAND

FROM WAVES POUNDING BOULDERS IN POURING RAIN TO THE SMELL OF A TURF FIRE

TO WALKING THROUGH SPRAY BLOWING OFF KYLEMORE LOUGH TO A LOW TIDE LINE

TO THE HIGHEST POINT OF THE WALK TO A CAMP UNDER FAST CLOUDS AND A FULL MOON

TO THE FIRST SUN AT 76 MILES TO THE FLASH OF AN ELLIPTICAL CLOUD OF STARLINGS

TO A PALE ORANGE MOON RISING TO THE RIVER SHANNON SWIRLING INTO LOUGH REE

TO SNOWDROPS TO STRAIGHT ROADS UNDULATING TO THE HORIZON TO TURF CUTTINGS

TO GETTING WATER FROM A WELL TO A GLIMPSE OF A STAR BETWEEN CLOUDS TO CROSSING A PEAT BOG

TO LYING NEAR THE ROADSIDE WATCHING CLOUDS MOVING ACROSS THE SKY FROM WEST TO EAST

TO A CLOSE WORLD IN MORNING MIST TO FACING MAGNETIC NORTH TO A FOSSIL TO A FLAT IRISH SEA

A WALK OF 221 MILES IN 7 DAYS FROM THE WEST COAST TO THE EAST COAST WINTER 1998

MIDWINTER NIGHT'S WALK

BY THE LIGHT OF A FULL MOON ON THE WINTER SOLSTICE

A WALK OF 16 HOURS FROM SUNSET TO SUNRISE

SOMERSET ENGLAND 1999

WALKING TO A SOLAR ECLIPSE

STARTING FROM STONEHENGE

A WALK OF 235 MILES

ENDING ON A CORNISH HILLTOP

AT A TOTAL ECLIPSE OF THE SUN

1999

THE SPACE OF TIME

FROM A CIRCLE DRAWN IN SNOW ON THE SUMMIT OF COTOPAXI IN ECUADOR 1998
TO A CIRCLE DRAWN WITH WATER ON THE SUMMIT OF PARNASSUS IN GREECE 1999

210 DAYS BETWEEN THE CIRCLES

STONES ADDED TO A FIELD CIRCLE

A WALK OF SIX DAYS THROUGH THE MARITIME ALPS

FROM VILLANOVA IN ITALY TO ST-ÉTIENNE-DE-TINÉE IN FRANCE

AUTUMN 1999

TIME FLOWING AND TIME REPEATING

A WALK OF SIX DAYS THROUGH THE MARITIME ALPS
FROM VILLANOVA IN ITALY TO ST-ÉTIENNE-DE-TINÉE IN FRANCE

A COLUMN OF FLAT STONES WAS MADE ON THE FIRST PASS
THESE STONES WERE CARRIED FORWARD ON THE WALK
AND THE COLUMN WAS RE-MADE ON EACH PASS ALONG THE WAY
UNTIL THE COLUMN OF STONES WAS LEFT STANDING ON THE LAST PASS

COLLE SEILLIERE

PASSO DI VALLANTA

PASSO DELLA LOSETTA

COL DU LONGET

COL DU VALLONNET

COL DU MALLEMORT

PAS DE LA CAVALE

COL DES FOURCHES

COL DE LA COLOMBIÈRE

COL D'ANELLE

AUTUMN 1999

A WALK OF FLUX

FROM A RISING TIDE IN THE BRISTOL CHANNEL TO THUNDER CLOUDS FORMING

TO WALKING THROUGH A STREAM TO A WANING QUARTER MOON

TO CHANGING STATES OF MIND TO WALKING THROUGH A SHOWER OF RAIN

TO WATER TAKEN FROM THE RIVER BRUE CARRIED FOR 20 MILES AND POURED INTO THE RIVER NADDER

TO WALKING AROUND *SPRING ELLIPSE* IN SALISBURY – FROM ONE WORK TO ANOTHER

TO SLEEPING IN AN OLD MILL ABOVE THE SOUND OF THE MILLRACE TO FLOATING STICKS OVER A WEIR

TO A BADGER DECOMPOSING TO DAMMING A STREAM THEN RELEASING THE FLOW

TO DISSOLVING A LUMP OF EARTH INTO A RIVER TO A HIGH TIDE ON THE TURN IN THE SOLENT

A WALK OF FIVE DAYS ENGLAND 1999

WALKING FROM ONE MILLENNIUM TO ANOTHER

FROM THE LAST MIDDAY OF 1999 TO THE FIRST MIDDAY OF 2000

A WALK OF 80 MILES IN 24 HOURS

MIDNIGHT ON GLASTONBURY TOR IN SOMERSET ENGLAND

A TRAIL OF WATER CIRCLES

FOURTEEN NIGHTS CAMPING ALONG A WILDERNESS WALK

EACH MORNING AFTER BREAKING CAMP
A CIRCLE OF WATER
POURED AROUND MY SLEEPING PLACE
BEFORE WALKING ON

INYO NATIONAL FOREST CALIFORNIA 2000

A STONE LINE BEFORE A BLIZZARD

A FIFTEEN DAY WALK

INYO NATIONAL FOREST CALIFORNIA WINTER 2000

HICKORY WIND CIRCLE

DISTANCE AND TIME TIME AND DISTANCE

FOUR WALKS ON DARTMOOR

ONE WALK LEADS TO ANOTHER

FIRST DAY WALKING 28 MILES : 9 HOURS

SECOND DAY WALKING FOR 9 HOURS : $26\frac{1}{4}$ MILES

THIRD DAY WALKING $26\frac{1}{4}$ MILES : $8\frac{1}{2}$ HOURS

FOURTH DAY WALKING FOR $8\frac{1}{2}$ HOURS : 26 MILES

ENGLAND WINTER 2000

WALKING WITH FIVE STONES

WALKING ACROSS FIVE RIVERS

WALKING OVER FIVE TORS

WALKING AROUND FIVE BOGS

WALKING FOR FIVE DAYS

TURNING AROUND ALL POINTS

OF THE COMPASS COUNTLESS TIMES

ALONG THE WAY OF A FOOTPATH WALK

MARKING TIME WITH MUDDY FOOTPRINTS

A WALK OF THIRTEEN DAYS IN THE SWISS ALPS SUMMER 2000

GLACIER STONES
A 13 DAY MOUNTAIN WALK
BEGINNING AND ENDING IN LEUK
SWITZERLAND 2000

SUMMIT STONES

A 13 DAY MOUNTAIN WALK BEGINNING AND ENDING IN LEUK

SWITZERLAND 2000

BLACK RIVER CIRCLE
A TWELVE DAY WALK ON THE FORT APACHE INDIAN RESERVATION
ARIZONA 2000

APACHE CIRCLE

A WALK OF FIFTY MILES

A WALK OF SEVENTEEN HOURS

A WALK OF FOUR MILES AN HOUR

A WALK CARRYING A HUNDREDWEIGHT

FOUR WALKS OF KNOWN AND UNKNOWN FACTORS

WOOD TO WOOD

A WALK OF 220 MILES IN SEVEN DAYS LINKING OLD WOODLANDS OF WESSEX

A WALK FROM WOOD TO WOOD, PLANTING A NUT FROM ONE WOOD IN THE NEXT WOOD

FROM POWERSTOCK COMMON TO PUDDLETOWN FOREST

TO COOMBE WOOD TO WAREHAM FOREST

TO HOLT WOOD TO CRANBORNE CHASE

TO GROVELY WOOD TO THE NEW FOREST

TO LANGLEY WOOD TO BENTLEY WOOD

TO QUEEN ELIZABETH FOREST TO HAREWOOD FOREST

TO OAKHILL WOOD TO SAVERNAKE FOREST

ENGLAND AUTUMN 2001

HEAVEN AND EARTH

MOVING BY DAY RESTING BY NIGHT
GLACIER CREEK GLITTERING WATER GLITTERING OBSIDIAN
EACH SLEEPING PLACE THE DREAMS AT EACH SLEEPING PLACE
NORTH SISTER KICKING IN SNOW-STEPS *WICKIUP PLAIN* EASY WALKING
AN ODD NUMBER OF MOUNTAINS AN EVEN NUMBER OF RIVERS
THE EARTH'S AXIS MAGNETIC NORTH POSITIVE MAGNETIC SOUTH NEGATIVE
THE WALK AS A TRUE PATH SOME FALSE MOVES

A 15 DAY WALK IN THE THREE SISTERS WILDERNESS OREGON 2001

DEAD WOOD CIRCLE
A 15 DAY WALK IN THE THREE SISTERS WILDERNESS
OREGON 2001

SISTERS STONES

HIGHLAND TIME

A WINTER WALK OF SEVENTEEN DREAMS

CROSSING CREAG DHUBH CAIRN AT A MIDDAY

FROM A BLIZZARD TO A FULL MOON RISING

WHILE THE EARTH TRAVELS 5,740,000 MILES IN ITS ORBIT

SCOTLAND 2002

NATURAL FORCES

WALKING WITH THE FORCE OF GRAVITY

IN THE FORCE OF THE WIND

THROUGH THE FORCE OF RIVERS

ALONG MAGNETIC FORCE BY COMPASS

OVER GEOLOGICAL FORCE ON THE STICKLEPATH FAULT

A FOUR DAY WINTER WALK ON DARTMOOR 2002

PHENOMENA

FROM A HIGH TIDE TO THE VERNAL EQUINOX SUNSET

FROM APPLE BLOSSOM TO QUARTZ CONGLOMERATE

FROM A CUMULUS CLOUD TO A RIVER SOURCE

FROM FIRST MOONLIGHT TO A FOX BARK

FROM A BLACK LAMB TO A BIRD'S NEST

FROM A SUNRISE TO A LOW TIDE

A WALK OF FIVE DAYS AND ONE NIGHT IN AVON ENGLAND 2002

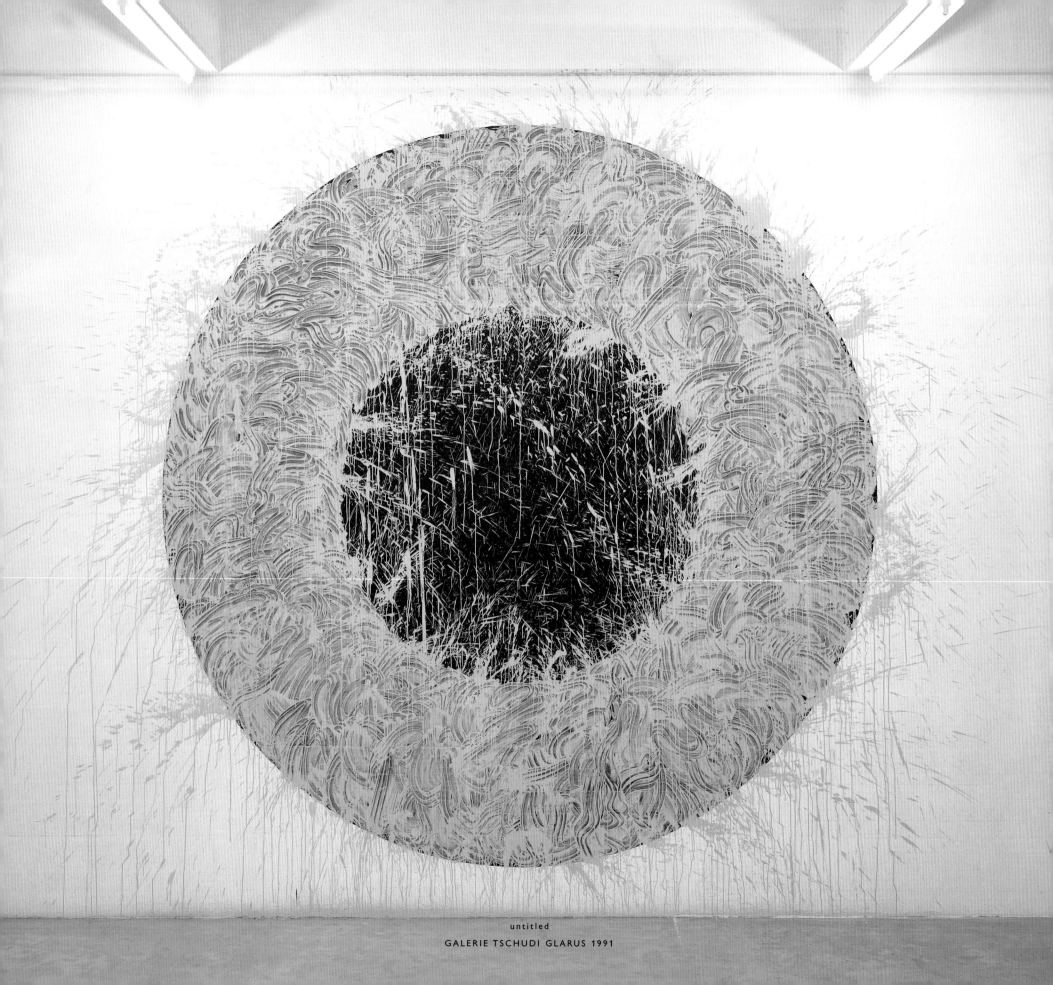

untitled
GALERIE TSCHUDI GLARUS 1991

EXHIBITIONS

PLANET CIRCLE

THE HAYWARD GALLERY LONDON 1991

SUMMER CIRCLE
THE HAYWARD GALLERY LONDON 1991

CORNWALL CIRCLE

THE HAYWARD GALLERY LONDON 1991

THAMES CIRCLES

THE HAYWARD GALLERY LONDON 1991

RIVER AVON MUD CIRCLE
THE HAYWARD GALLERY LONDON 1991

A LINE THE LENGTH OF A STRAIGHT WALK FROM THE BOTTOM TO THE TOP OF SILBURY HILL (1970)
THE HAYWARD GALLERY LONDON 1991

WHITE WATER CIRCLE
SPERONE WESTWATER NEW YORK 1991

RAINFOREST LINE
SPERONE WESTWATER NEW YORK 1991

EARTHQUAKE CIRCLE

GALERIE TSCHUDI GLARUS 1991

RIVER AVON MUD CIRCLE

JEAN BERNIER ATHENS 1992

CORNWALL CHINA CLAY CIRCLE

LOS ANGELES 1992

ORCADIAN CIRCLE

DUBLIN 1992

CONTINENTS CIRCLES
FUNDACIO ESPAI POBLENOU BARCELONA 1992

HOGWALLOW FLAT CIRCLE
STONY MAN CIRCLE
HAZELTOP CIRCLE
65 THOMPSON STREET NEW YORK 1993

CORNWALL SLATE LINE (1990)
ARC-MUSÉE D'ART MODERNE DE LA VILLE DE PARIS 1993

BARK CIRCLE

ARC-MUSÉE D'ART MODERNE DE LA VILLE DE PARIS 1993

THE RIVERS OF FRANCE

ARC-MUSÉE D'ART MODERNE DE LA VILLE DE PARIS 1993

STONE GROUND

[illegible text block]

KOREA SPRING 1993

小 白 山

MIDSUMMER CIRCLES
ANTHONY d'OFFAY GALLERY LONDON 1993

FOOTPRINT SPIRAL
ANTHONY d'OFFAY GALLERY LONDON 1993

MUDDY WATER WALL AND RING OF WHITE MARBLE
GALERIE TSCHUDI GLARUS 1993

WHITE WATER CIRCLE AND
NEANDERTAL LINE (detail)
KUNSTSAMMLUNG NORDRHEIN-WESTFALEN DÜSSELDORF
1994

RED MUD CIRCLE

SPERONE WESTWATER NEW YORK 1994

TIERRA DEL FUEGO CIRCLE   SANTA CRUZ CIRCLE   CHUBUT CIRCLE
SPERONE WESTWATER NEW YORK 1997

RED MUD CIRCLES

PALAZZO DELLE ESPOSIZIONI ROME 1994

ROMULUS CIRCLE AND REMUS CIRCLE
PALAZZO DELLE ESPOSIZIONI ROME 1994

ROME CIRCLE
PALAZZO DELLE ESPOSIZIONI ROME 1994

MUDDY WATER LINE

PALAZZO DELLE ESPOSIZIONI ROME 1994

217

MUDDY WATER CIRCLE

PALAZZO DELLE ESPOSIZIONI ROME 1994

MUDDY WATER CIRCLE

PALAZZO DELLE ESPOSIZIONI ROME 1994

RED AND GREY MUD WALL
TUCCI RUSSO STUDIO PER L'ARTE CONTEMPORANEA TORRE PELLICE ITALY 1994

WHITE RIVER LINE
SÃO PAULO BIENAL BRAZIL 1994

MOJAVE BONE CIRCLE
LAURA CARPENTER FINE ART SANTA FE 1995

CORNWALL SUMMER CIRCLE

ANTHONY d'OFFAY GALLERY LONDON 1995

WHITE HAND GROUND LINE
KONRAD FISCHER DÜSSELDORF 1995

CIRCLE OF TIME STICKS AND CIRCLE OF MEMORY STICKS
KONRAD FISCHER DÜSSELDORF 1995

SETAGAYA MUD LINE AND SETAGAYA CIRCLE
SETAGAYA ART MUSEUM TOKYO 1996

HEMISPHERE CIRCLE
THE TOKYO FORUM TOKYO 1996

PUGET SOUND DRIFTWOOD CIRCLE
CONTEMPORARY ARTS MUSEUM HOUSTON 1996

RIVER AVON DRIFTWOOD CIRCLE
WILHELM LEHMBRUCK MUSEUM DUISBURG 1996

SEA MILLS DRIFTWOOD CIRCLE

ANTHONY d'OFFAY GALLERY LONDON 1996

FROM ONE TO ANOTHER AND HOUSTON CIRCLE
CONTEMPORARY ARTS MUSEUM HOUSTON 1996

GULF OF MEXICO ARC   PUJET SOUND DRIFTWOOD CIRCLE
RING OF FLINT   TEXAS CIRCLE   HOUSTON CIRCLE

GLARUS ARC AND GLARUS LINE
GALERIE TSCHUDI GLARUS 1996

BERLIN CIRCLE
HAMBURGER BAHNHOF MUSEUM FÜR GEGENWART BERLIN 1996

CIRCLE OF LIFE
SPAZIO ZERO PALERMO 1997

PUJET SOUND MUD CIRCLE

HENRY ART GALLERY UNIVERSITY OF WASHINGTON SEATTLE 1997

BLACK WHITE GREEN PINK PURPLE CIRCLE
GALERIE TSCHUDI GLARUS 1998

PERIPHERY STONES

ORANGERIE KUNSTVEREIN HANNOVER 1999

WHITE WATER LINES

PLATONIC WALKS

A STRAIGHT LINE   A CIRCLE   AN ELLIPSE

THREE WALKS MADE ON DARTMOOR EACH TEN MILES LONG

THE TIME DIFFERENCE BETWEEN THE FASTEST AND THE SLOWEST WALK 28 MINUTES

ENGLAND 1999

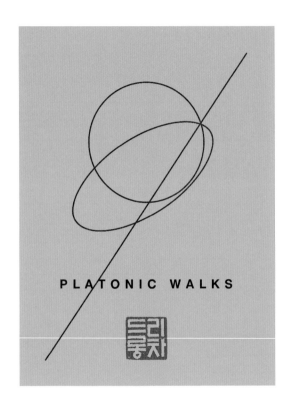

PLATONIC WALKS

THE INVITATION CARD FOR AN EXHIBITION AT
BERNIER/ELIADES ATHENS 1999
AND THE INSTALLED TEXT WORK

ΠΛΑΤΩΝΙΚΟΙ ΠΕΡΙΠΑΤΟΙ

ΕΥΘΕΙΑ   ΚΥΚΛΟΣ   ΕΛΛΕΙΨΗ

ΤΡΕΙΣ ΠΕΡΙΠΑΤΟΙ ΣΤΟΝ ΚΑΜΠΟ ΤΟΥ DARTMOOR ΔΕΚΑ ΜΙΛΙΑ Ο ΚΑΘΕΝΑΣ

Η ΔΙΑΦΟΡΑ ΧΡΟΝΟΥ ΜΕΤΑΞΥ ΤΟΥ ΠΙΟ ΓΡΗΓΟΡΟΥ ΚΑΙ ΤΟΥ ΠΙΟ ΑΡΓΟΥ ΠΕΡΙΠΑΤΟΥ 28 ΛΕΠΤΑ

ΑΓΓΛΙΑ 1999

FAST HAND MUD ARC
BERNIER/ELIADES ATHENS 1999

RED MUD ELLIPSE
TUCCI RUSSO STUDIO PER L'ARTE CONTEMPORANEA TORRE PELLICE ITALY 1998

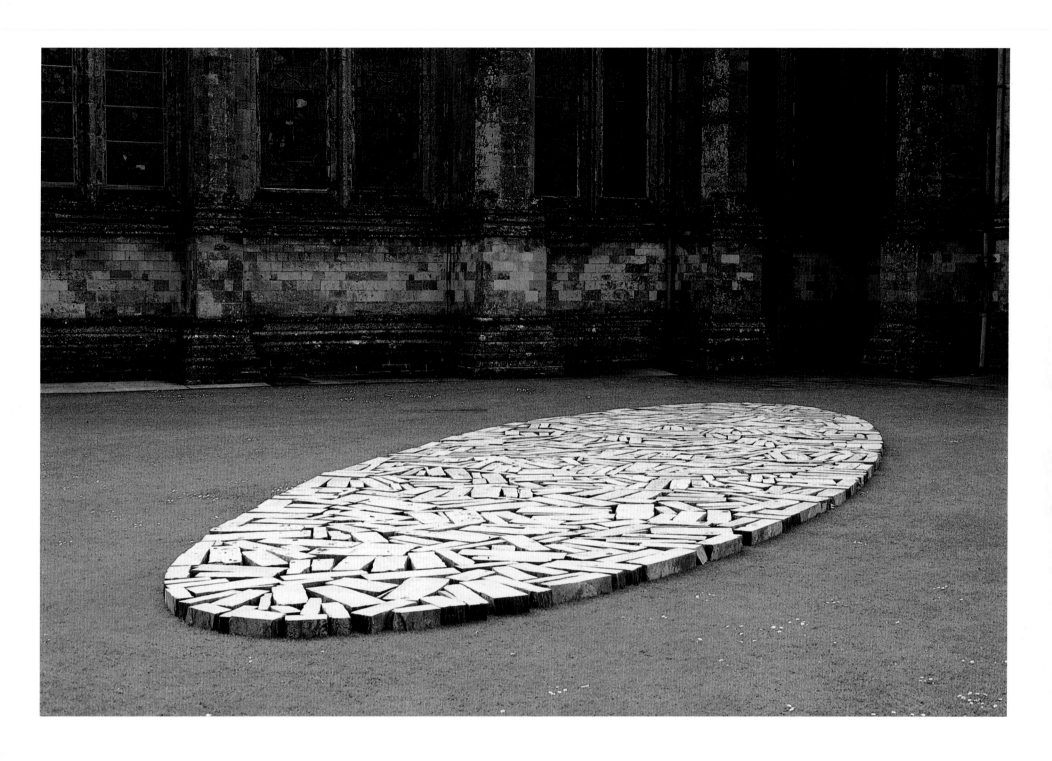

SPRING ELLIPSE

SALISBURY CATHEDRAL 1999

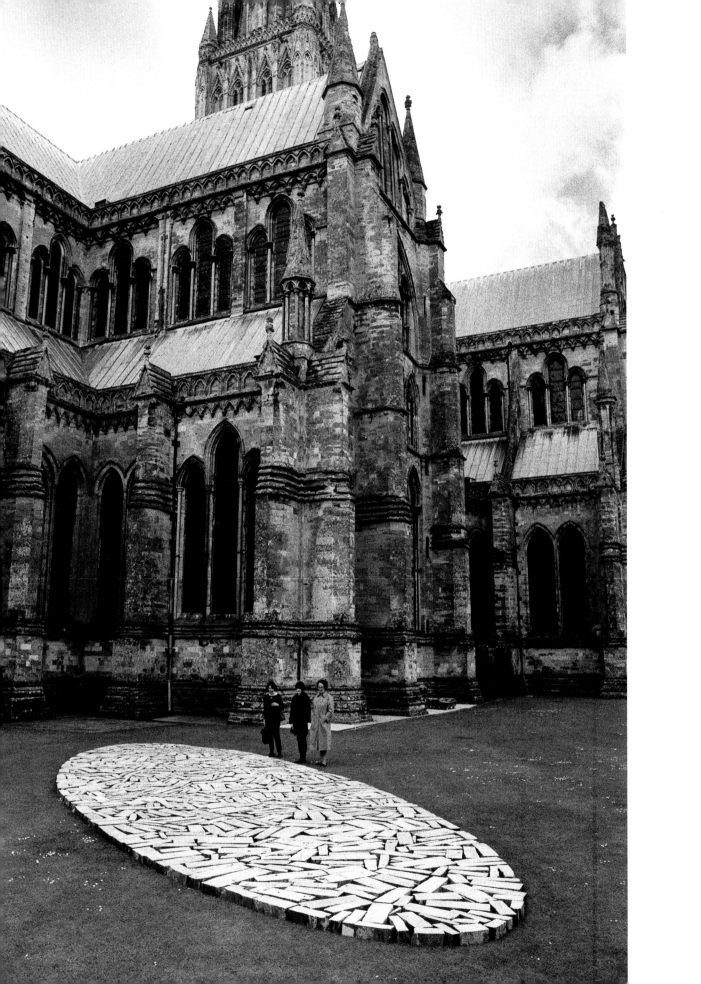

A footpath is a place.

It also goes from place to place, from here to there, and back again.

Any place along it is a stopping place.

Its perceived length could depend on the speed of the traveller, or its steepness, or its difficulty.

Reversing direction does not reverse the travelling time.

A path can be followed, or crossed.

A path is practical: it takes the line of least resistance, or the easiest, or most direct, route.

Sometimes it can be the only line of access through an area.

Paths are shared by all who use them.

Each user could be on a different overall journey, and for a different reason.

Animals also make use of human trails, and vice versa.

A path is made by movement, by the accumulated footprints of its users.

Paths are maintained by repeated use, and would disappear without use.

The characteristics of a path depend upon the nature of the land, but the characteristics can be universal.

A long walk is often made by joining a selection of different paths together, one to another, to make one particular journey.

There is an infinite and cosmic variety of journeys, at all scales.

Around the world in different cultures, paths are marked in many different ways, with cairns, signposts, milestones, prayer flags, shrines, menai walls, and other sacred or cultural markers.

FOOTPATH LINE
ISLA DE ESCULTURAS PONTEVEDRA SPAIN 1999

ANTIBES ELLIPSE
CHANTIER NAVAL OPÉRA ANTIBES 1999

ENERGY AXIS
GALERIA MÁRIO SEQUEIRA BRAGA PORTUGAL 1999

BROWNSTONE CIRCLE

SEAGRAM PLAZA NEW YORK 2000

WHITE QUARTZ ELLIPSE

DORIS C. FREEDMAN PLAZA NEW YORK 2000

CORNWALL SLATE ELLIPSE
SPERONE WESTWATER NEW YORK 2000

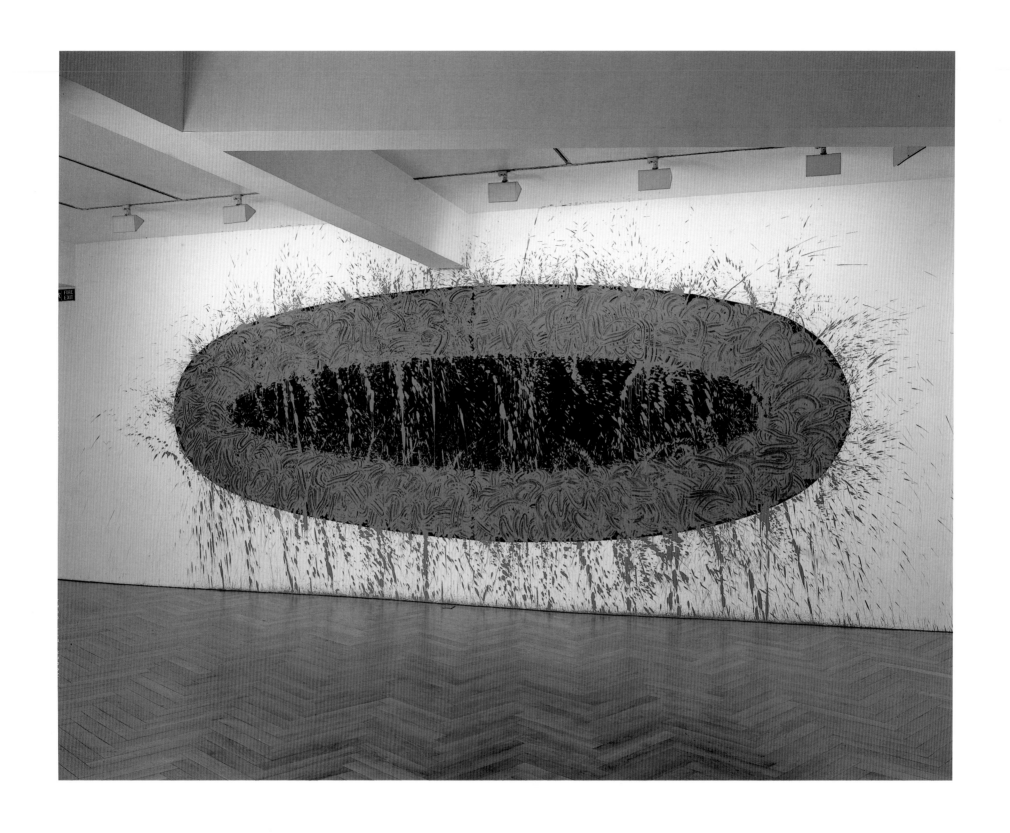

RIVER AVON MUD ELLIPSE

ANTHONY d'OFFAY GALLERY LONDON 2000

RIVER AVON MUD ARC

BILBAO GUGGENHEIM 2000

RHÔNE VALLEY MUD HAND CIRCLES

SCHLOSS LEUK SWITZERLAND 2000

RHÔNE VALLEY STONES SPIRAL
SCHLOSS LEUK SWITZERLAND 2000

NORTH SOUTH EAST WEST CIRCLES
SCHLOSS LEUK SWITZERLAND 2000

A LINE OF CIRCLES

MILWAUKEE ART MUSEUM 2001

SCIROCCO CIRCLE

PANTELLERIA SICILY 2000

PORFIDO ELLIPSE
MUSEUM OF MODERN ART PALAZZO DELLE ALBERE TRENTO 2000

WHITE MUD ELLIPSE
MUSEUM OF MODERN ART PALAZZO DELLE ALBERE TRENTO 2000

TRENTO ELLIPSE
MUSEUM OF MODERN ART PALAZZO DELLE ALBERE TRENTO 2000

BASALT ELLIPSE
MUSEUM KURHAUS KLEVE 2001

BIRD DROPPING FINGERPRINT CIRCLE STONE 1990

MAKING FINGERPRINT STONES

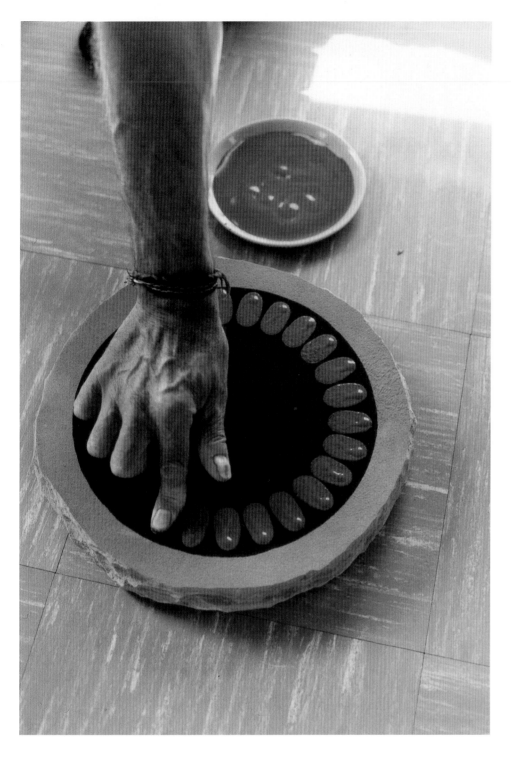

FINGERPRINT STONE

JAMES COHAN GALLERY NEW YORK 2000

FINGERPRINT STONE

2000 FINGERPRINTS

RIVER AVON MUD GRIFFIN CONTEMPORARY LOS ANGELES 2000

CHINA CLAY ON AFRICAN WOOD

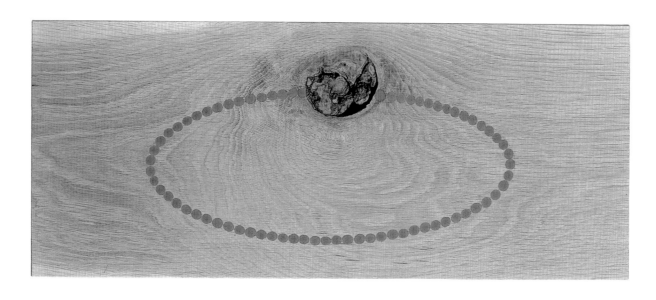

RIVER AVON MUD ON OAK

RIVER AVON MUD ON AFRICAN WOOD

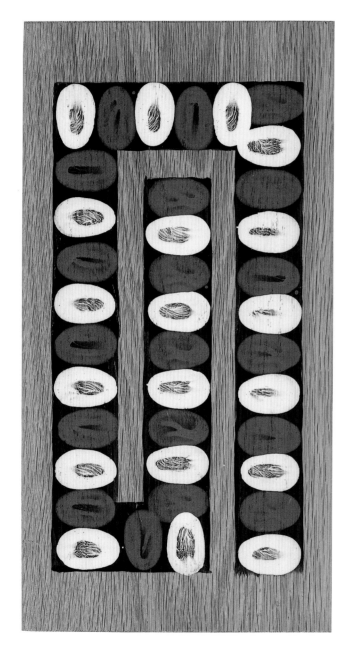

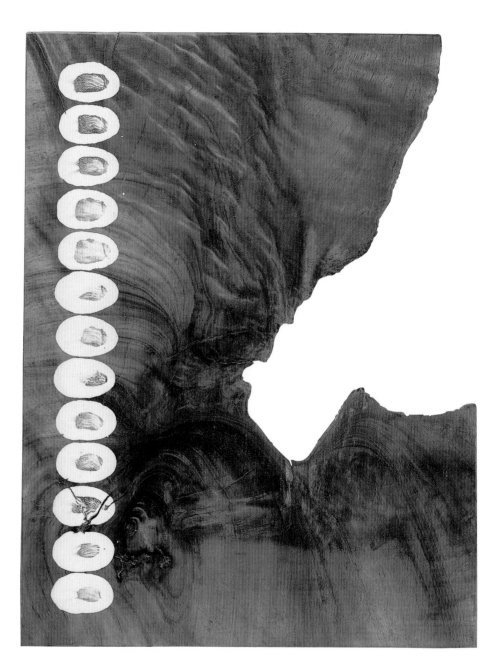

RIVER AVON MUD AND CHINA CLAY ON OAK

CHINA CLAY ON HAWAIIAN WOOD

277

MAKING RIVER AVON MUD WORKS ON RIVER AVON DRIFTWOOD

GALERIE TSCHUDI GLARUS SWITZERLAND 2000

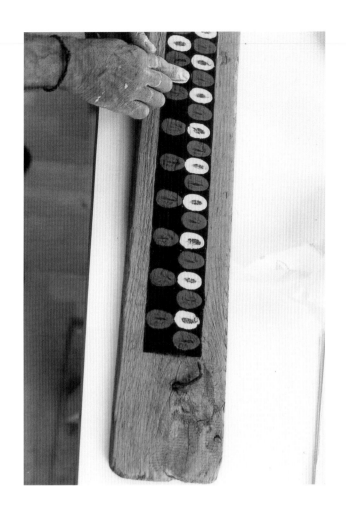

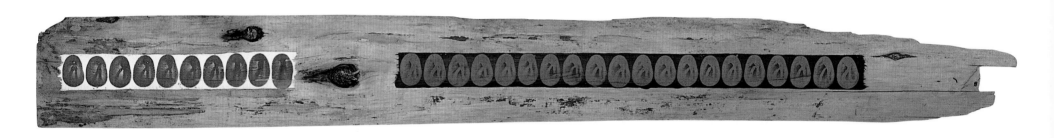

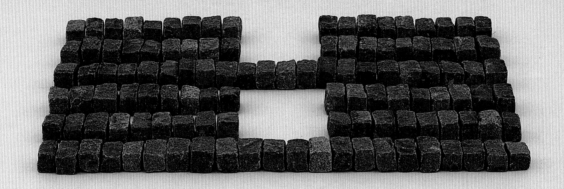

FOLLOWING
THUNDER
TRANQUILLITY

GALERIA MÁRIO SEQUEIRA BRAGA PORTUGAL 2001

EARTH CIRCLE AND BRAGA MUD ELLIPSE
MUSEU SERRALVES PORTO 2001

INSTALLATION VIEWS MUSEUM KURHAUS KLEVE 2001

RIVER AVON MUD AND CHINA CLAY WALL 2001

FORTE DI VINADIO
CIRCLE
ITALY 2001

HEAVEN
GALERIE TSCHUDI GLARUS 2002

EARTH
GALERIE TSCHUDI GLARUS 2002

HEAVEN AND EARTH CIRCLE

RIVERS

DARTMOOR RIVERBED STONES

R I V E R   T O   R I V E R
S T O N E   T O   S T O N E

A 2½ DAY WALK AROUND THE EDGE OF DARTMOOR

A STONE FROM THE RIVER BOVEY CARRIED TO THE RIVER WEBBURN

A STONE FROM THE RIVER WEBBURN CARRIED TO THE RIVER DART

A STONE FROM THE RIVER DART CARRIED TO HOLY BROOK

A STONE FROM HOLY BROOK CARRIED TO THE RIVER MARDLE

A STONE FROM THE RIVER MARDLE CARRIED TO DEAN BURN

A STONE FROM DEAN BURN CARRIED TO THE RIVER AVON

A STONE FROM THE RIVER AVON CARRIED TO THE RIVER ERME

A STONE FROM THE RIVER ERME CARRIED TO THE RIVER YEALM

A STONE FROM THE RIVER YEALM CARRIED TO THE RIVER PLYM

A STONE FROM THE RIVER PLYM CARRIED TO THE RIVER MEAVY

A STONE FROM THE RIVER MEAVY CARRIED TO THE RIVER WALKHAM

A STONE FROM THE RIVER WALKHAM CARRIED TO THE RIVER TAVY

A STONE FROM THE RIVER TAVY CARRIED TO THE RIVER LYD

A STONE FROM THE RIVER LYD CARRIED TO THE RIVER LEW

A STONE FROM THE RIVER LEW CARRIED TO THE RIVER OKEMENT

A STONE FROM THE RIVER OKEMENT CARRIED TO THE RIVER TAW

A STONE FROM THE RIVER TAW CARRIED TO THE RIVER TEIGN

A STONE FROM THE RIVER TEIGN CARRIED TO THE RIVER BOVEY

ENGLAND SPRING 1991

W A T E R S H E D

RIVER AVON TO RIVER THAMES

A WALK OF 120 MILES IN 39 HOURS FROM BRISTOL BRIDGE TO LONDON BRIDGE

A DAY NIGHT DAY NIGHT WALK

ENGLAND 1992

HIGH TIDE TO HIGH TIDE

RIVER MEDWAY TO RIVER SEVERN

A WALK OF 173 MILES IN SEVEN AND A HALF TIDES

FROM HIGH TIDE ON THE RIVER MEDWAY (LOW TIDE ON THE RIVER SEVERN)
TO HIGH TIDE ON THE RIVER SEVERN (LOW TIDE ON THE RIVER MEDWAY)

EAST COAST TO WEST COAST ENGLAND 1992

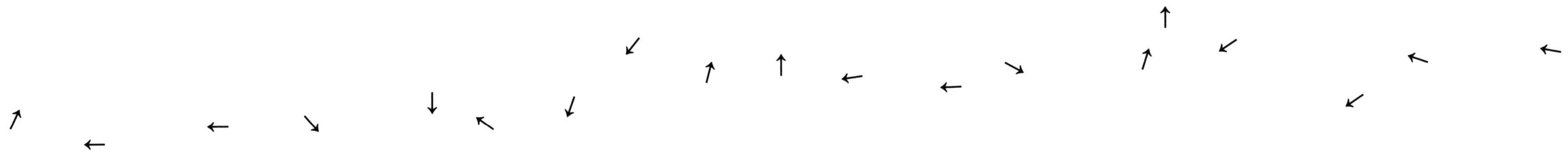

WIND LINE WALK

FROM THE GARONNE TO THE PO

THE DIRECTION OF THE WIND NOTED WHEN CROSSING THE RIVER GARONNE
AND ONCE EACH DAY UNTIL CROSSING THE RIVER PO

A WALK OF 586 MILES IN 18 ½ DAYS FROM BORDEAUX TO TURIN

FRANCE AND ITALY AUTUMN 1992

RIO GRANDE CANYON STONES

THROWING STONES INTO THE RIVER

ON AN 8 DAY SOUTHWARD WALK FOLLOWING THE WESTERN RIM OF THE RIO GRANDE CANYON

WALKING FROM THE BEGINNING OF THE CANYON TO WHERE THE RIVER HAS CUT IT 650 FEET DEEP

THE FIRST STONE THROWN AT WATER LEVEL AND THE OTHERS THROWN FROM THE EDGE OF THE CLIFFS
DOWN INTO THE RIVER AT INCREASING HEIGHTS UNTIL THE LAST STONE AT THE END OF THE WALK

COLORADO AND NEW MEXICO 1993

SPLASH SPLASH SPLASH SPLASH
SPLASH
SPLASH
SPLASH
SPLASH
SPLASH
SPLASH
SPLASH
SPLASH

WATER WALK

A COAST TO COAST WALK FROM THE IRISH SEA TO THE NORTH SEA
A WALK OF 349 MILES IN 11 DAYS CARRYING WATER TO WATER

WATER FROM CARDIGAN BAY POURED INTO THE AFON RHEIDOL

WATER FROM THE AFON RHEIDOL POURED INTO THE RIVER WYE

WATER FROM THE RIVER WYE POURED INTO THE RIVER ITHON

WATER FROM THE RIVER ITHON POURED INTO THE RIVER LUGG

WATER FROM THE RIVER LUGG POURED INTO THE RIVER TEME

WATER FROM THE RIVER TEME POURED INTO THE RIVER SEVERN

WATER FROM THE RIVER SEVERN POURED INTO THE RIVER ARROW

WATER FROM THE RIVER ARROW POURED INTO THE RIVER AVON

WATER FROM THE RIVER AVON POURED INTO THE RIVER CHERWELL

WATER FROM THE RIVER CHERWELL POURED INTO THE RIVER TOVE

WATER FROM THE RIVER TOVE POURED INTO THE RIVER GREAT OUSE

WATER FROM THE RIVER GREAT OUSE POURED INTO THE RIVER CAM

WATER FROM THE RIVER CAM POURED INTO THE RIVER LARK

WATER FROM THE RIVER LARK POURED INTO THE RIVER WAVENEY

WATER FROM THE RIVER WAVENEY POURED INTO THE NORTH SEA

WALES AND ENGLAND 1999

WHITE RIVER BLACK RIVER

A CAMP AT THE FORK ALONG A 12 DAY WALK FOLLOWING AND BETWEEÑ BOTH RIVERS ON THE FORT APACHE INDIAN RESERVATION ARIZONA 2000

CONTINUUM WALK

WATER TAKEN FROM THE MOUTH OF THE RIVER DART
CARRIED ON A CONTINUOUS WALK OF THIRTEEN HOURS
AND POURED INTO THE HEADWATERS OF THE RIVER AT ITS SOURCE

DEVON ENGLAND 1998

AVON TO AVON TO AVON

A HUNDRED MILE WALK IN THREE DAYS

FROM THE RIVER AVON IN HAMPSHIRE

TO THE RIVER AVON IN WILTSHIRE

TO THE RIVER AVON IN WARWICKSHIRE

ENGLAND 2001

RIVER TO WOOD

WOOD TO TOR

TOR TO RIVER

RIVER TO TOR

TOR TO WOOD

WOOD TO RIVER

EAST DART RIVER WISTMAN'S WOOD SITTAFORD TOR

A WALK ON DARTMOOR WINTER 2001

RIVER PO LINE

AZEGLIO THE PO VALLEY NORTHERN ITALY 2001

EXCERPTS FROM *STEPPING STONES*

a conversation with Denise Hooker

DH: I've heard you say that your work is a portrait of yourself in the world, your engagement with it by walking, and the interaction of your energy with the materials and forces of nature. I know you see your work as coming from the concerns of your generation of artists, but it also seems to stem from your childhood and the landscape in which you grew up. There's a duality in your art between travelling far and staying close to your roots. It's both a record of where you've gone and where you've come from.

RL: Yes. The story of home and away. My first memory of landscape was my grandfather's cottage at Lustleigh in Devon. The garden went down to a gate that opened directly on to this big clear river which was the river Dart. My parents met in a rambling club, which is strange but true. I used to go hitch-hiking with my dad and on cycling and youth-hostelling holidays with him as a boy. He was a primary teacher and every year he would take his inner-city kids on a day's walk, which became a tradition, and I would go with them. Everyone would meet at the Suspension Bridge and spend the day walking down the river on the towpath to Pill, which was the village where the pilots lived who navigated the ships up the River Avon. We would get the ferry across the river at Pill and come back to Bristol on the train.

DH: Why was that outing so important to you?

RL: With the hindsight of me making art from walking, I can now see it as my father sharing his love of nature and walking in the local places with me and his schoolchildren. Every year he would take the family to see the spring tides at Pill. The Bristol Channel has the second highest tides in the world, and he would take us down to see the flooded or sandbagged houses in the main street, so I guess he was really interested in the tides.

The only object I remember making as a child was a model of a river with plaster of Paris in a baking tin. It had mud banks and creeks at different levels with little inlets coming into it which I slowly filled up with water and emptied to make the tide come in and out.

DH: How old would you have been then?

RL: I suppose nine or ten. At the same time as my friends were making model aeroplanes, which I had no interest in doing, I made this river in the baking tin.

DH: The tides became an important theme in your later work.

RL: I suppose one of the themes of my work is measurement: measurement between distance and walking time, or distance and stones, or places to sea level. I once made a walk of the same length as the River Avon along the Foss Way Roman road. *Water Walk* is about the particular number of rivers I crossed on my route along a walk from Cardigan Bay to the North Sea. I have found many ways to measure myself in relation to the landscape. Most of the longer walks I was measuring by days and nights, or sometimes the solar cycle of twenty-four hours. Then I had the idea that a walk could also be measured by lunar time, and as the moon makes the tides, I could measure a walk by the tide. So I did *Tide Walk*. An important line in that text work is 'relative to the walker'. Because the tide is a wave which travels round the coast, the tide times are not synchronised between the English Channel and the Bristol Channel. So that walk was very much about relativity, in that the tide will always be in a different state from the point of view of the start of the walk compared to the end of it. It was like measuring the walk with two different clocks. And of course the tides make the mud, so the Avon is an infinite source of all that wonderful material for me, not to mention the driftwood.

DH: People rarely appear in your work. There are occasional references to them in your text works, but *Nomad Circle* is the only photograph of a landscape work to include a person in it.

RL: Well, it's unusual, and it happened by chance. I was making a circle in Mongolia and out of the corner of my eye I could see this herdsman following his sheep and goats as they grazed nearer and nearer. Finally he came up and asked for a cigarette. I don't smoke, but we had a chat, as one does, even without a common language. As we were standing in my circle I asked if I could do a photo, which I did as he made a roll-up. By which time he had to go and catch up his animals. My two Mongolian friends were some way off, making a campfire. It had been too windy to put up the tents, or more accurately there was no sheltered place. They were cooking a huge fish which had been caught in a lake. I beckoned the man over, and we all ate this fish around the fire. It was still too windy to put up a tent, so he invited us to spend the night with him in his ger (the circular Mongolian nomad's tent). He had his young son and teenage daughter with him; his wife was visiting relatives. It was an almost biblical experience, with the day's end ritual of rounding up the animals, putting only the young ones into flimsy wicker pens, the girl milking the yaks and goats, the boy watering the horses; then spending the evening on beautiful carpets around the fire in the tent, watching the man carefully bind up the broken leg of a sheep between two bits of firewood. And it was my birthday. That's just a rich example of how a work can sometimes be the tip of the iceberg of anecdotal experience, which may inform, but is not really the subject of the work, which was a sculpture. I'm anyway an opportunist in finding the places for sculptures, and the man was a unique and unforeseen bonus who defined that circle at that moment and gave it its title.

DH: Just recently, in the last year or so, there seem to be big changes in your work. You've started to use the Chinese I Ching symbols – for heaven, earth, and mountain, for instance. What do they mean to you?

RL: Well, I'd had this big I Ching book for a while, and then I realised what beautiful visual images the hexagrams made. So it started there, and then I was doing a show in Paris, and I knew I couldn't really get good natural stones there so I had the idea to use pavés, the granite cobblestones typical of the Paris streets. I was looking at these geometric images and it was practical to use these geometric stones, so they seemed perfect for each other. Another aspect of the I Ching hexagrams is that they are halfway between being an abstract image and a text work, because although they are not language, they do have a meaning. And the symbols have really strong, epic, classic meanings like Wind, Tranquillity, Transience, Change, which give them a power and a strength.

DH: So they're a move away from your use of universal forms like the circle?

RL: I suppose so, yes.

DH: And you've been using them both in your sculpture and your mud works.

RL: Yes. For me they're interchangeable. The photos, the walks, the sculptures, the text works, they're all just formal variations, just different ways of sort of doing the same thing all the time.

DH: Another important formal change in your sculpture lately is that the circle has been broken.

RL: Yes. But it's just another way of doing a circle. I had the idea seeing a natural-looking broken circle in the landscape, maybe a patch on a hillside with a jagged path or an animal track going through it, or whatever. On that walk with you in the Piemonte on September 11.

DH: Given that the circle is such a resonant symbol, what's the significance of dividing the circle?

RL: There's no symbolism. With symbolism there's a fixed meaning. All good art is open-ended, not a closed system. People can bring their own interpretations to it. Or not. Stones are what they are.

In my work the circle is given a particular meaning by my having used it in many different ways over the years. It's a pure idea which can take the form of a walk, mud, wind, water, words, or stones…

DH: It's quite a potent image to break the circle.

RL: It is, yes, but on the other hand I would say I'm making a path, a walking line through the circle so a person can cross it as well as walk around it. In a way it goes back to my student plaster path in the studio in Bristol, or my walking line, or the various negative spaces that make some of my landscape works. So now one can walk through a sculpture.

DH: You're inviting us in.

RL: Yes, to see a circle in a different way.

DH: In what way?

RL: Well, you can now be in the middle looking out rather than outside pissing in.

London 11 May 2002

BREAKING CAMP MOVING ON

Richard Long was born in Bristol, England, 2 June 1945. He studied at the West of England College of Art, Bristol, from 1962 to 1965, and at St. Martin's School of Art, London, from 1966 to 1968. Among other distinctions, he was winner of the Turner Prize, Tate Gallery, London, in 1988. He lives and works in Bristol.

Richard Long has made walks in Algeria, Argentina, Australia, Bolivia, Canada, Ecuador, England, Finland, France, Greece, Iceland, India, Ireland, Italy, Japan, Kenya, Korea, Malawi, Mexico, Mongolia, Morocco, Nepal, Norway, Peru, Portugal, Scotland, The Seychelles, Spain, Sweden, Switzerland, Tanzania, Turkey, United States, Wales and Zambia.

ONE-MAN EXHIBITIONS

1968
Düsseldorf, Konrad Fischer, 'Sculpture', 21 September – 18 October.

1969
New York, John Gibson, 'Richard Long', 22 February – 14 March.
Düsseldorf, Konrad Fischer, 'Richard J. Long', 5 July – 1 August.
Krefeld, Museum Haus Lange, 'Richard Long: Exhibition One Year', July 1969 – July 1970.
Paris, Galerie Yvon Lambert, 'Sculpture', 5 – 26 November.
Milan, Galerie Lambert, 'A Sculpture by Richard Long', 15 November – 1 December.

1970
Düsseldorf, Konrad Fischer, 'Eine Skulptur von Richard Long', 11 May – 9 June.
Mönchengladbach, Städtisches Museum, '4 Sculptures', 16 July – 30 August.
New York, Dwan Gallery, 'Richard Long', 3 – 29 October.

1971
Turin, Gian Enzo Sperone, 'Richard Long', opened 13 April.
Amsterdam, Art & Project, 'A Sculpture by Richard Long', 17 July – 6 August.
London, Whitechapel Art Gallery, 'Richard Long', 9 – 21 November.
Oxford, Museum of Modern Art, 'Richard Long', 9 – 23 December.

1972
New York, Museum of Modern Art, 'Projects: Richard Long', 14 March – 17 April.
Paris, Galerie Yvon Lambert, 'Look the Ground in the Eye', opened 3 May.

1973
London, Lisson Gallery, 'Richard Long', 23 January – 24 February.
Antwerp, Wide White Space, 'Richard Long', 5 March – 12 April.
Düsseldorf, Konrad Fischer, 'A Rolling Stone', 29 March – 25 June.
Amsterdam, Stedelijk Museum, 'Richard Long', 7 December 1973 – 27 January 1974.

1974
New York, John Weber Gallery, 'Richard Long', 4 – 29 May.
Edinburgh, Scottish National Gallery of Modern Art, 'Richard Long', 9 July – 11 August.
London, Lisson Gallery, 'Richard Long', 1 – 30 November.
Düsseldorf, Konrad Fischer, 'River Avon Driftwood', 20 December 1974 – 19 January 1975.

1975
Amsterdam, Art & Project, 'River Avon Driftwood, Crossing Two Rivers / Minnesota / Wiltshire', 18 March – 5 April.
Antwerp, Wide White Space, 'Driftwood', 15 April – 16 May.
Paris, Galerie Yvon Lambert, 'Richard Long', 24 April – 20 May.
Basel, Rolf Preisig, 'Richard Long', 12 June – 12 July.
Plymouth, Plymouth School of Art, 'Richard Long', date unknown.

1976
Rome, Gian Enzo Sperone, 'Stone Circles', 16 March – April.
Düsseldorf, Konrad Fischer, 'River Avon Driftwood', 15 May – 11 June.
Antwerp, Wide White Space, 'Richard Long', 25 May – 10 June.
London, Lisson Gallery, 'Stones', 24 – 26 June.
Venice, XXXVII Venice Biennale, British Pavilion, 'Richard Long', 18 July – 10 October.
Tokyo, Art Agency Co. Ltd., 'Richard Long', opened 14 October.
Bristol, Arnolfini, 'River Avon Driftwood', 23 November – 24 December.
New York, Sperone Westwater Fischer, 'Richard Long', 4 December 1976 – 8 January 1977.

1977
London, Whitechapel Art Gallery, 'Richard Long', 25 January – 27 February.
Amsterdam, Art & Project, 'A Stone Sculpture by Richard Long', 8 February – 5 March.
Poznan, Galeria Akumulatory 2, 'Kamienne Kolo', 9 May – 19 June.
Basel, Rolf Preisig, 'Richard Long', 17 May – 21 June.
London, Lisson Gallery, 'Richard Long', 21 May – 18 June.
Berne, Kunsthalle Bern, 'Richard Long', 15 July – 7 August.
Melbourne, National Gallery of Victoria, 'Richard Long', 8 December 1977 – 7 January 1978.
Sydney, Art Gallery of New South Wales, 'John Kaldor Art Project 6: Richard Long', 16 December – 5 February 1978.

1978
Amsterdam, Art & Project, 'Driftwood Circle', 10 January – 4 February.
Paris, Yvon Lambert, 'Richard Long', 2 February – 3 April.
Düsseldorf, Konrad Fischer, 'Richard Long', 11 March – 7 April.
London, Lisson Gallery, 'Outback', 2 – 20 May.
Leeds, Park Square Gallery, 'Richard Long', 6 – 30 June.
Zürich, Halle für internationale neue Kunst, 'Richard Long', 19 July – 31 August.
New York, Sperone Westwater Fischer, 'Richard Long', 30 September – 21 October.

Hamburg, Ausstellungsraum Ulrich Rückriem, 'Richard Long', 21 October – 12 November.

1979
Zürich, Halle für internationale neue Kunst, 'Richard Long', 19 February – 8 April.
London, Anthony d'Offay, 'The River Avon', 15 March – 12 April.
Basel, Rolf Preisig, 'Richard Long', 6 April – 5 May.
Londonderry, Orchard Gallery, 'Recent Work by Richard Long', 1 – 19 May.
Southampton, University Gallery, University of Southampton, 'Chalk Stone Line 1979', 11 – 29 June.
Eindhoven, Stedelijk Van Abbemuseum, 'Sculpturen en Fotowerken', 29 September – 28 October.
London, Lisson Gallery, 'Richard Long', 9 October – 9 November.
Tokyo, Art Agency Co. Ltd., 'Richard Long', 20 October – 16 November.
Oxford, Museum of Modern Art, 'Richard Long', 11 November – 23 December.

1980
Athens, Karen & Jean Bernier, 'Stone Circles', 1 – 29 March.
Amsterdam, Art & Project, 'Stones and Sticks', 22 March – 19 April.
Cambridge, Massachusetts, Fogg Art Museum, Harvard University, 'Richard Long', 17 April – 1 June.
New York, Sperone Westwater Fischer, 'Richard Long', 26 April – 17 May.
London, Anthony d'Offay, 'New Work', 17 September – 16 October.
Düsseldorf, Konrad Fischer, 'Richard Long', 8 – 29 November.

1981
New York, Sperone Westwater Fischer, 'Richard Long', 10 – 31 January.
Edinburgh, Graeme Murray Gallery, 'Black and White Willow Circles', 7 – 28 February.
Zürich, Konrad Fischer, 'Richard Long', 8 May – 6 June.
London, Anthony d'Offay, 'Richard Long', 3 June – 8 July.
Toronto, David Bellman Gallery, 'New Work', 12 September – 10 October.

Bordeaux, Centre d'Arts Plastiques Contemporains de Bordeaux, 'Richard Long', 4 December 1981 – 30 January 1982.

1982
Amsterdam, Art & Project, 'Richard Long', 23 January – 20 February.
Paris, Yvon Lambert, 'Richard Long', 13 February – 12 March.
Venice, Flow Ace Gallery, 'Richard Long', 1 – 31 May.
New York, Sperone Westwater Fischer, 'Richard Long', 25 September – 23 October.
Ottawa, National Gallery of Canada, 'Richard Long', 21 October 1982 – 9 January 1983.

1983
Toronto, David Bellman Gallery, 'Canadian Sculptures', 19 March – 16 April.
Bristol. Arnolfini, 'Selected Works 1965 – 1983', 26 March – 7 May.
London, Anthony d'Offay, 'New Works', 29 March – 12 May.
Tokyo, Century Cultural Foundation, 'Richard Long Exhibition', 18 April – 31 May.
Tokyo, Art Agency Tokyo, 'Richard Long', 20 April – 31 May.
Turin, Antonio Tucci Russo, 'Richard Long', 20 May – 30 September.
Düsseldorf, Konrad Fischer, 'Richard Long', 16 September – 14 October.

1984
London, Coracle Press, 'Watermarks', 7 – 31 January.
Naples, Lucio Amelio, 'Stone', 14 January – 6 February.
Paris, Galerie Crousel-Hussenot, 'New Works', 10 March – 15 April.
Athens, Jean Bernier, 'Richard Long', 29 March – 28 April.
New York, Sperone Westwater, 'Richard Long', 5 May – 2 June.
Kilkenny, Butler Gallery, 'Richard Long', 25 August – 23 September.
Londonderry, Orchard Gallery, 'River Avon Mud Works', 23 September – 13 October.
London, Anthony d'Offay, 'Muddy Water Falls', 16 October – 16 November.
Düsseldorf, Konrad Fischer, 'Richard Long', 20 October – 30 November.

1985
Basel, Galerie Buchmann, 'Richard Long', 26 January – 9 March.
London, Anthony d'Offay, 'From Pass to Pass', 4 – 29 June.
Kendal, Abbot Hall Art Gallery, 'Richard Long', 6 July – 1 September.
Malmö Konsthall, 'Richard Long', 20 September – 13 October, 26 October – 24 November.
Milan, Padiglione d'Arte Contemporanea di Milano, 'Richard Long', 29 November 1985 – 25 February 1986.

1986
Madrid, Palacio de Cristal, 'Richard Long', 28 January – 20 April.
Paris, Galerie Crousel-Hussenot, 'Œuvres Récentes', 12 April – 13 May.
New York, Sperone Westwater, 'Richard Long', 6 – 16 September.
New York, Solomon R. Guggenheim Museum, 'Richard Long', 12 September – 30 November.
London, Anthony d'Offay Gallery, 'New Works', 8 October – 12 November.
Pori, Finland, Porin Taidemuseo, 'Richard Long', 4 December 1986 – 25 January 1987.
Turin, Antonio Tucci Russo, 'Richard Long', 12 December 1986 – 14 March 1987.

1987
Geneva, Musée Rath, 'Richard Long', 7 May – 21 June.
Liverpool, Renshaw Hall, 'Allotment One: Richard Long – Stone Fields', 19 May – September.
Chicago, Donald Young Gallery, 'Richard Long', 23 October – 28 November.
Nailsworth, Gloucestershire, Cairn Gallery, 'Cairn', 7 November – 5 December.
Grenoble, Centre National d'Art Contemporain de Grenoble, 'Richard Long', 13 December 1987 – 9 January 1988.
Athens, Jean Bernier, 'Richard Long', 15 December 1987 – 9 January 1988.

1988
Düsseldorf, Konrad Fischer, 'Richard Long', 20 February – end of March.
Aachen, Neue Galerie Sammlung Ludwig, '3. Kunstpreis Aachen', 14 October – 20 November.

London, Anthony d'Offay Gallery, 'Richard Long', 22 October – 26 November.

1989
St. Gallen, Switzerland, Kunstmuseum St. Gallen, 'Richard Long', 15 January – 26 February.
Athens, Jean Bernier, 'Richard Long', 23 February – 27 March.
New York, Sperone Westwater, 'Richard Long', 18 March – 15 April.
Bristol, Coopers Gallery, Old Vic Theatre, 'Footprints', 14 April – 27 May.
Turin, Galleria Tucci Russo, 'Richard Long', 21 April – 20 July.
Chagny, France, Galerie Pietro Sparta, 'Richard Long', 10 June – 1 October.
La Jolla Museum of Contemporary Art, 'Richard Long', 20 August – 15 October.
Halifax, The Henry Moore Sculpture Trust Studio, 'New Works', 25 October – 10 December.

1990
Bristol, Arnolfini, 'Richard Long', 20 January – 25 February.
London, Anthony d'Offay Gallery, 'Water and Stones', 26 January – 24 February.
Santa Monica, Angles Gallery, 'New Work', 23 March – 31 April.
Glarus, Switzerland, Galerie Tschudi, 'Richard Long', 7 July – 30 September.
Düsseldorf, Konrad Fischer, 'Turf Line', 14 July – mid-August.
London, Tate Gallery, 'Richard Long', 3 October 1990 – 6 January 1991.
Stockholm, Magasin 3 Stockholm Konsthall, 'Richard Long', 5 October 1990 – 30 January 1991.
Rochechouart, Musée Départemental d'Art Contemporain de Rochechouart, 'Richard Long', 11 October 1990 – 6 January 1991.

1991
Liverpool, Tate Gallery, 'Richard Long', 23 January – 3 March.
Frankfurt, Städtische Galerie im Städel, 'Richard Long', 21 February – 12 May.
Turin, Antonio Tucci Russo, 'Richard Long', 27 February – 27 April.

London, Hayward Gallery, 'Walking in Circles', 14 June – 11 August.
New York, Sperone Westwater, 'Richard Long', 19 October – 16 November.
Glarus, Galerie Tschudi, 'Richard Long', 23 November 1991 – May 1992.
Edinburgh, Scottish National Gallery of Modern Art, 'Stone Line 1980 and Selected New Works', December 1991 – February 1992.

1992
Athens, Jean Bernier, 'Richard Long', 23 January – 21 March.
Santa Monica, Angles Gallery, 'Mississippi Mud', 9 April – 9 May.
Barcelona, Fundació Espai Poblenou, 'Richard Long', 9 June – November.
Düsseldorf, Konrad Fischer, 'Richard Long', 7 November – 2 December.

1993
New York, 65 Thompson Street, 'Richard Long', 30 January – 13 March.
Paris, Musée d'Art Moderne de la Ville de Paris, 'River to River', 25 March – 29 May.
Seoul, Inkong Gallery, 'Richard Long', 23 April – 19 June.
London, Anthony d'Offay Gallery, 'Wayside Stones', 25 June – 12 August.
Santa Fe, Center for Contemporary Arts of Santa Fe, 'Richard Long', 22 October 1993 – 7 January 1994.
Glarus, Galerie Tschudi, 'Richard Long', 4 December – 8 December, 18 January – 28 May 1994.

1994
Düsseldorf, Konrad Fischer, 'Shenandoah Neandertal', 3 March – 5 April.
Düsseldorf, Kunstsammlung Nordrhein-Westfalen, 'Richard Long', 5 March – 24 April.
New York, The Public Library, 'Books, Prints, Printed Matter', 26 March – 25 June.
New York, Sperone Westwater, 'Richard Long', 26 March – 23 April.
Philadelphia Museum of Art, 'Museum Studies 2', 12 April – 7 August.
Rome, Palazzo delle Esposizioni, 'Richard Long', 4 May – 30 June.

Stromness, Orkney, The Pier Arts Centre, 'Richard Long', 17 June – 9 July.
Torre Pellice, Italy, Tucci Russo, 'Richard Long', 1 October 1994 – March 1995.
São Paulo, 22nd Bienal Internacional de São Paulo, 'Richard Long', 12 October – 11 December.
Sydney, Museum of Contemporary Art, 'Stones, Clay, Water', 21 December 1994 – 13 February 1995.

1995
Santa Fe, Laura Carpenter Fine Art, 'New Work', 1 March – 22 April.
Huesca, La Sala de Exposiciones de la Diputación de Huesca, 'Richard Long', 26 May – 10 September.
Reykjavik, Onnur Hæd Syningarsalur, 'Richard Long', July – August.
London, Anthony d'Offay Gallery, 'A Walk in Iceland, A Circle of Slate, A Walk in New Mexico', 12 September – 14 October.
San Francisco, Daniel Weinberg Gallery, 'Richard Long', 2 November 1995 – 13 January 1996.
Düsseldorf, Konrad Fischer, 'Walking Stones', 16 December – 21 December 1995, 9 January – 6 February 1996.

1996
Tokyo, Setagaya Art Museum, 'Richard Long Exhibition', 1 February – 24 March.
Kyoto, National Modern Art Museum, 'Richard Long Exhibition', 23 April – 26 May.
Houston, Contemporary Arts Museum, 'Circles, Cycles, Mud, Stones', 27 April – 30 June.
Fort Worth, The Annex of the Modern Art Museum of Fort Worth, 'Cornwall Summer Circle', 5 May – 7 July.
Bolzano, Galerie Museum / Galleria Museo, 'Dolomite Stones', 11 October – 30 November.
Glarus, Galerie Tschudi, 'Richard Long', 29 October – 14 December.
Exeter, Spacex Gallery, 'Dartmoor Time', 26 November – 21 December.

1997
Duisburg, Wilhelm Lehmbruck Museum, 'Richard Long', 19 January – 30 March.
St. Andrews, The Crawford Arts Centre, 'A Road from the Past to the Future', 21 March – 20 April.

Leeds, The Henry Moore Institute, 'More and Less;
The Early Work of Richard Long', 1 May – 13 July.
Naoshima, Bennesse House / Naoshima Contemporary
Art Museum, 'Richard Long', opened 25 May.
New York, Sperone Westwater, 'Richard Long',
20 September – 8 November.
Palermo, Spazio Zero-Cantieri Culturale alla Zisa,
'Richard Long', 1 November 1997 – 15 January 1998.
Bristol, City Museum & Art Gallery,
'Richard Long', 20 December 1997 – 31 March 1998.

1998
Zugspitze, Kunsthalle Zugspitze-Gipfelstation,
'Richard Long', 18 January – 14 June.
London, Anthony d'Offay Gallery, 'Richard Long',
28 April – 18 June.
Wakefield, Yorkshire Sculpture Park, 'Richard Long',
11 June – 6 September.
Glarus, Galerie Tschudi, 'Richard Long', 27 June –
5 September.
Torre Pellice, Tucci Russo, 'Richard Long',
19 September 1998 – 28 February 1999.

1999
Hanover, Kunstverein Hannover and Orangerie,
'Every Grain of Sand', 17 January – 14 March.
Athens, Bernier / Eliades, 'Platonic Walks', 4 March –
21 April.
Braga, Portugal, Galeria Mário Sequeira,
'Crossing the Duzon', 22 May – 31 July.
Cleves, Museum Kurhaus Kleve, 'Being in the
Moment', 4 December 1999 – 16 January 2000.

2000
Venice, Griffin, 'Two Thousand Fingerprints',
22 January – 4 March.
London, Anthony d'Offay Gallery, 'Richard Long',
18 February – 11 March.
New York, Sperone Westwater, 'The Time of Space',
1 – 29 April.
New York, James Cohan Gallery, 'Fingerprint
Stones', 5 April – 13 May.
New York, The Public Art Fund, 'Richard Long:
New York Projects', 12 April – June.
Bristol, Royal West of England Academy,
'Richard Long', 21 May – 8 July.
Bilbao, Guggenheim Museum, 'Richard Long',
24 June – 15 October.

Leuk, Schloss Leuk, 'Richard Long im Schloss Leuk',
20 August – 21 October.
Trento, Museo d'Arte Moderna e Contemporanea di
Trento e Rovereto, 'Richard Long', 2 September –
5 November.
Düsseldorf, Konrad Fischer Galerie, 'Richard Long',
14 October 2000 – 27 January 2001.
Glarus, Galerie Tschudi, 'River Avon Mud on River
Avon Driftwood', 2 – 23 December, 16 January –
17 February 2001.

2001
Paris, Galerie Daniel Templon, 'Mountain', 26 April –
26 May.
Cleves, Museum Kurhaus Kleve, 'Richard Long',
24 June – 23 September.
Porto, Museu Serralves, 'Heaven and Earth',
20 October 2001 – 6 January 2002.
Milwaukee, Milwaukee Art Museum, 'On Site:
Richard Long', 14 November 2001 – 3 March 2002.

2002
Venice, Griffin Contemporary, '02 02 02', 2 February –
2 April.
Glarus, Galerie Tschudi, 'Richard Long', 16 February –
31 May.
East Wintersloe, nr. Salisbury, Roche Court, New
Art Centre, Sculpture Park & Gallery, 'Richard
Long', 18 May – 22 September.
St. Ives, Tate St. Ives, 'A Moving World', 13 July –
13 October.

SELECTED GROUP EXHIBITIONS

1967
Frankfurt, Galerie Loehr, '19:45 – 21:55', from
9 September.

1968
London, Royal Institute Galleries, 'Young
Contemporaries', 30 January – 27 February.
Amalfi, Festival of Free Expression, 'A3: Arte e
Azione Povera', October.

1969
Ithaca, New York, Andrew Dickson White Museum
of Art, Cornell University, 'Earth Art', 11 February –
16 March.
New York, Seth Siegelaub, 'One Month', March.
Amsterdam, Stedelijk Museum, 'Op Losse Schroeven',
15 March – 27 April.
New York, John Gibson, 'Ecologic Art', 17 May –
June.
New York, Seth Siegelaub, 'July, August, September
1969', July – September.
Berne, Kunsthalle Bern, 'Live in your head – when
attitudes become form', 22 March – 27 April; travelled
to Krefeld, Museum Haus Lange, 10 May – 25 June,
and London, Institute of Contemporary Arts,
24 September – 27 October.
Düsseldorf, Städtische Kunsthalle, 'Prospect 69',
30 September – 12 October.
Amalfi, 'RA 4, Azioni Povera', 4 – 6 October.

1970
Humlebæck, Louisiana Museum, 'Tabernakel',
24 January – 22 February.
Chicago, Museum of Contemporary Art, 'Evidence
on the Flight of Six Fugitives', 28 March – 10 May.
Paris, Rue Mouffetard, '18 Paris IV 70', April.
New York, Museum of Modern Art, 'Information',
2 July – 20 September.

1971
New York, The Solomon R. Guggenheim Museum,
'Guggenheim International Exhibition 1971',
12 February – 25 April.
New York, The New York Cultural Center,
'The British Avant Garde', I 9 May – 29 August.
Wuppertal, Von der Heydt-Museum, 'Fünf Sammler –
Kunst unserer Zeit', 5 June – 11 July.
Arnhem and other locations in the Netherlands,
'Sonsbeek 71, Sonsbeek buiten de perken', 19 June –
15 August.

1972
New York, John Weber Gallery, 'De Europa',
29 April – 24 May.
Kassel, Neue Galerie and Museum Fridericianum,
'Documenta V', 30 June – 8 October.
London, Hayward Gallery, 'The New Art',
17 August – 24 September.
Paris, Yvon Lambert, 'Actualité d'un Bilan', October.

1973
Rome, Parcheggio di Villa Borghese, 'Contemporanea', November 1973 – February 1974.

1974
Brussels, Palais des Beaux-Arts, 'Carl Andre, Marcel Broodthaers, Daniel Buren, Victor Burgin, Gilbert & George, On Kawara, Richard Long, Gerhard Richter', 9 January – 3 February.
London, Royal College of Art, 'Sculpture Now: Dissolution or Redefinition', 11 – 22 November.

1975
Lucerne, Kunstmuseum Luzern, 'Spiralen & Progressionen', 16 March – 20 April.
Bristol, Arnolfini, 'Artists Over Land', 26 August – 20 September.
Otterlo, Rijksmuseum Kröller-Müller, 'Funkties van tekenen / Functions of drawing', 25 May – 4 August.

1976
Milan, Palazzo Reale, 'Arte Inglese Oggi 1960 – 1976', 26 February – 16 May.
Washington, Corcoran Gallery of Art, 'Andre / Le Va / Long', 11 December 1976 – 30 January 1977.

1977
Los Angeles Institute of Contemporary Art, 'Michael Asher, David Askevold, Richard Long', 15 January – 10 February.
New York, The Fine Arts Building, 'British Artists', 5 February – 1 March.
Münster, 'Skulptur', 3 July – 13 November.
Dublin, National Museum of Ireland and Hugh Lane Gallery of Modern Art, 'ROSC '77, the poetry of vision', 21 August – 30 October.
Washington, Hirshhorn Museum and Sculpture Garden, 'Probing the Earth: contemporary land projects', 27 October 1977 – 2 January 1978; travelled to La Jolla Museum of Contemporary Art, 27 January – 26 February 1978, and Seattle Art Museum, 23 March – 21 May 1978.

1978
Newlyn Art Gallery, Cornwall, 'Peter Joseph, Richard Long, David Tremlett in Newlyn', 17 January – 17 February.

London, Coracle Press, 'Fo(u)ndlings, 1978', 22 April – 9 June.
Bordeaux, capcCentre d'Arts Plastiques Contemporains de Bordeaux, 'Sculpture / Nature', 5 May – 1 July.

1979
Paris, Musée d'Art Moderne de la Ville de Paris, 'Un Certain Art Anglais…', 19 January – 12 March.
London, Hayward Gallery, 'Hayward Annual, 1979', 19 June – 27 August.
Berne, Kunsthalle Bern, 'Skulptur: Matisse, Giacometti, Judd, Flavin, Andre, Long', 17 August – 23 September.

1980
Humlebæck, Louisiana Museum, 'Andre, Dibbets, Long, Ryman', 19 January – 24 February.
London, Hayward Galery, 'Pier + Ocean', 8 May – 22 June; travelled to Otterlo, Rijksmuseum Kröller-Müller, 13 July – 8 September.
St. Ives, Summer Festival, 'Roger Ackling, Hamish Fulton, Richard Long, Michael O'Donnell: Four Temporary Works Situated in West Penwith, Cornwall, England', September.
Sheffield, Mappin Art Gallery, 'Artist and Camera', 25 October – 23 November.
London, Coracle Press, 'On Loan', 22 November – 19 December.

1981
Zürich, Kunsthaus Zürich, 'Mythos & Ritual in der Kunst der 70er Jahre', 5 June – 23 August
Toyama, The Museum of Modern Art, 'For a New Art: Toyama Now '81', 5 July – 23 September.
London, Anthony d'Offay, 'New Work', 25 July – 22 August.
Stuttgart, Württembergischer Kunstverein, 'Natur-Skulptur', 1 September – 1 November.
London, Whitechapel Art Gallery, 'British Sculpture in the 20th Century. Part 2: Symbol and Imagination, 1951 – 1980', 27 November 1981 – 24 January 1982.

1982
Hamburg, Halle 6 in der Kampnagel-Fabrik, 'Objekt, Skulptur, Installation', May – June.
London, Anthony d'Offay, 'Gilbert & George, Richard Long. Bruce McLean', 19 May – 18 June.

Berlin, Nationalgalerie Staatliche Museen Preussischer Kulturbesitz, 'Kunst wird Material', 7 October – 5 December.
Kassel, 'Documenta 7', 19 June – 28 September.

1983
London, Anthony d'Offay, 'Works on Paper', 19 July – 26 August.
Helsinki, Ateneum, 'ARS 83', 14 October – 11 December.

1984
New Haven, Yale Center for British Art, 'The Critical Eye / 1', 16 May – 15 July.
Bordeaux, capcMusée d'Art Contemporain, 'Légendes', 19 May – 9 September.
Raleigh, North Carolina Museum of Art, 'Gilbert & George / Richard Long', 9 June – 9 September.
Ercolano, Villa Campolieto, 'Terrae Motus', 6 July – 31 December.
Dublin, The Guinness Hop Store, 'ROSC '84: the poetry of vision', 24 August – 17 November.
Cambridge, Kettle's Yard Gallery, '1965 to 1972 – when attitudes became form', 14 July – 2 September; travelled to Edinburgh, Fruitmarket, 6 October – 17 November.
Otterlo, Rijksmuseum Kröller-Müller, 'Kleine Arena / Little Arena', 13 October – 25 November.

1985
Perth, Art Gallery of Western Australia, 'The British Show', 19 February – 24 March; travelled to Sydney, Art Gallery of New South Wales, 23 April – 9 June, and Brisbane, Queensland Art Gallery, 5 July – 11 August.
Turin, Castello di Rivoli, 'Ouverture', 18 December – end of 1986.

1986
Madrid, Palacio de Velázquez, 'Entre el Objeto y la Imagen', 28 January – 20 April.
Bremen, Kunstverein Bremen, 'Bodenskulptur', 29 April – 15 June.
Cambridge, Kettle's Yard Gallery, 'Landspace: place, nature, material', 12 July – 31 August.
München, Städtische Galerie im Lenbachhaus, 'Beuys zu Ehren', 16 July – 2 November.

1987
Scottish Art Council touring exhibition, 'The Unpainted Landscape', 10 January – 15 November. Travelled to Ayr, Maclaurin Art Gallery; Stromness, Pier Arts Centre; Edinburgh, Scottish National Gallery of Modern Art; Aberdeen, Artspace Galleries; Glasgow, Collins Gallery; St. Andrews, Crawford Centre for the Arts; Bristol, Arnolfini.
London, Royal Academy of Arts, 'British Art in the 20th Century: The Modern Movement', 15 January – 5 April.
Tampere, Finland, Sara Hildén Art Museum, 'Britannia, paintings and sculptures from the 1980s', 16 June – 23 August.
Manchester, Cornerhouse, 'Wall Works: Richard Long, Michael Craig-Martin, Annette Messager, Marion Möller, Matt Mullican, Sol LeWitt – Six artists working directly on the wall', 14 November – 31 December.
Chicago, Museum of Contemporary Art, 'A Quiet Revolution: British Sculpture since 1965', 31 January – 5 April; travelled to San Fransisco, Museum of Modern Art, 4 June – 26 July.

1988
Liverpool, Tate Gallery, 'Starlit Waters: Brittish Sculpture, An International Art 1968 – 1988', 28 May – 4 September.
Reykjavik, The Living Art Museum, 'Donald Judd, Richard Long, Kristján Gudmundsson', 4 – 19 June.
Cambridge, Jesus College, 'Sculpture in the Close', 20 June – 31 July.
Saint Louis, The Saint Louis Art Museum, 'New Sculpture / Six Artists', 23 September – 30 October.
Nailsworth, Cairn Gallery, 'In Praise of Walking', 8 October – 9 November.

1989
Cologne, Rheinhallen der Kölner Messe, 'Bilderstreit', 8 April – 28 June.
Paris, Centre Pompidou / La Grande Halle – La Vilette, 'Magiciens de la Terre', 18 May – 14 August.
Berlin, Hamburger Bahnhof, 'Zeitlos', 22 June – 25 September.
Saint Etienne, Musée d'art moderne, 'Collection Panza: Richard Long, Bruce Nauman', 30 June – 6 September.

Furkapasshöhe, Hotel Furkablick, 'Furkart', July – September.
Istanbul, Süleymaniye Cultural Centre, '2. Istanbul Bienali', 25 September – 31 October.

1990
Oslo, Wang Kunsthandel, '3 + 1: Paul Brand, Terje Roalkvam, Dag Skedsmo, Richard Long', 13 January – 11 February.
Vienna, Messepalast, 'Von der Natur in der Kunst', 3 May – 15 July.
Lincoln, Lincoln Cathedral, 'The Journey', 17 June – 12 August
Bordeaux, capcMusée d'art contemporain de Bordeaux, 'Collection: Christian Boltanski, Daniel Buren, Gilbert & George, Jannis Kounellis, Sol Lewitt, Richard Long, Mario Merz', 29 June – 30 December.
Paris, Galerie Ghislaine Hussenot, 'Time, Space, Place: Richard Long, On Kawara, Lawrence Weiner', 8 September – 18 October.

1991
Madrid, Galeria Weber, Alexander y Cobo, 'Hamish Fulton, Richard Long', 6 February – 30 March.
London, Anthony d'Offay Gallery, 'Bronze, Steel, Stone, Wood: Carl Andre, Ellsworth Kelly, Richard Long', March – April.
Geneva, Cabinet des Estampes du Musée d'art et d'histoire, 'Midi-Minuit: Richard Long, Markus Raetz', 26 November – 8 December.

1992
London, Anthony d'Offay Gallery, 'New Work on Paper: Richard Long, Gerhard Richter, Lawrence Weiner', 5 February – 8 March.
Klagenfurt, Kunsthalle Ritter, 'Shapes and Positions', 11 September 1992 – 30 January 1993; travelled to Kassel, Museum Fridericianum, 14 February – 18 April 1993.
Cases de Pène, Château de Jau / Collioure, Musée d'art moderne de Collioure, 'Exposition sentimentale: Wolfgang Laib, Richard Long, Richard Serra, Lawrence Weiner', 26 June – 30 September.
Tilburg, Stichting De Pont, 'De Opening', 13 September 1992 – 31 January 1993.

1993
London, Hayward Gallery, 'Gravity and Grace', 21 January – 14 March.
London, Lissson Gallery, 'Out of Sight Out of Mind', 15 February – 3 April.
Krefeld, Museum Haus Lange / Museum Haus Esters, 'Künstler Bücher 1', 28 February – 12 April.
Rochechouart, Musée départemental d'art contemporain de Rochechouart, 'La Collection', 10 April – 13 June.
Otterlo, Rijksmuseum Kröller-Müller, 'Over het landschap / About landscape', 28 August – 24 October.

1994
London, Anthony d'Offay Gallery, 'Painting, Drawing & Sculpture', 2 March – 8 April.
Eindhoven, Peninsula, 'Dear Stieglitz', 1 May – 26 June.
Porto, Fundação de Serralves, 'Arca de Noé / Noah's Ark', 29 November 1994 – 19 February 1995.
London, Anthony d'Offay Gallery, 'Sculpture', 6 December 1994 – 14 February 1995.

1995
Maastricht, Bonnefantenmuseum, 'Sculptuur uit de collectie Marlies en Jo Eyck', 11 March – 3 September.
Amsterdam, Stedelijk Museum, 'Art & Project: De Amsterdamse Jaren 1968 – 1989', 18 March – 23 April.
Santiago de Compostella, Auditorio de Galicia, 'Escultura Británica Contemporánea: De Henry Moore a los años 90', 10 June – 30 July; travelled to Porto, Fundação de Serralves, 7 September – 5 November.
Vienna, Galerie nächst St. Stephan, 'Donald Judd and his artist friends', 22 September – 18 November.

1996
London, Anthony d'Offay Gallery, 'Portrait of the Artist', April – June.
Bristol, The Old Leadworks, 'Swinging the Lead', 24 May – 22 June.
Cambridge, Jesus College, 'Sculpture in the Close, Quincentenary Exhibition', 22 September – 29 October.
Eindhoven, Van Abbemuseum and Peninsula, 'Travaux Publics / Public Works', 8 December 1996 – 9 February 1997.

1997
Antwerp, Openluchtmuseum voor beeldhouwkunst Middelheim, 'Wide White Space in Middelheim', 2 March – 17 August.
London, Anthony d'Offay Gallery, 'De Re Metallica', 5 June – 2 August.
Corte, FRAC Corse, 'Géographiques', 21 June – 13 September.

1998
Stuttgart, Staatsgalerie, 'On a clear day', 4 April – 21 June.
New York, John Weber Gallery, 'Land Marks', 13 September – 11 October.
New York, The Townhouse, 'An Exhibition for Children', 5 December – 22 December.

1999
London, The Walk Gallery, 'The Spirit of Mongolia', 8 May – 29 May.
Düsseldorf, Konrad Fischer Galerie, 'Walls / Wände', 8 May – 19 June.
Antibes, Chantier Naval Opéra, 'Richard Long, Sebastian Smith, Serge de Hildebrandt', 26 July – 3 September.

2000
London, Whitechapel Art Gallery, 'Live In Your Head: Concept and Experiment in Britain, 1965 – 1975', 4 February – 2 April.
Bristol, Failand Village Hall, 'Failand Village Arts, Crafts & Photography Exhibition', 25 June.

2001
Amiens, Fonds régional d'art contemporain de Picardie, 'Paysages', 12 May – 30 June.
Liverpool, Tate Liverpool, 'At Sea', 14 July – 23 September.

2002
The Moor Falmouth, Falmouth Art Gallery, 'Delabole, the Slate Quarry Show: Richard Long, Kurt Jackson', 4 January – 2 February.
Cambridge, Kettle's Yard, 'A Measure of Reality', 9 March – 28 April.
Breda, De Beyerd, '10 Nederlandse privé-collecties', 7 April – 26 May.
Amsterdam, Stedelijk Museum, 'Conceptual Art

1965 – 1975 from Dutch and Belgian Collections', 20 April – 23 June.

SELECTED PUBLICATIONS

1970
Richard Long Skulpturen. Text: Richard Long and Johannes Cladders. Städtisches Museum Mönchengladbach.

1971
Two sheepdogs cross in and out of the passing shadows. The clouds drift over the hill with a storm. Lisson Gallery, London.
From along a Riverbank. Art & Project, Amsterdam.

1973
John Barleycorn. Stedelijk Museum, Amsterdam.
South America. Konrad Fischer, Düsseldorf.
From around a Lake. Art & Project, Amsterdam.

1974
Inca Rock Campfire Ash. Scottish National Gallery of Modern Art, Edinburgh.

1977
The North Woods. Whitechapel Art Gallery, London.
A Hundred Stones. Kunsthalle Bern.
A Straight Hundred Mile Walk in Australia. John Kaldor Project 6, National Gallery of Victoria, Melbourne / Art Gallery of New South Wales, Sydney.

1978
Sydamerika. Kalejdoskop, Lund, Sweden.
Rivers and Stones. Newlyn Orion, Cornwall.

1979
River Avon Book. Anthony d'Offay, London.
A Walk Past Standing Stones. Anthony d'Offay, London.
Richard Long. Stedelijk Van Abbemuseum, Eindhoven.

1981
Twelve Works 1979 – 1981. Anthony d'Offay, London.

1982
Bordeaux 1981. Centre d'Arts Plastiques Contemporains de Bordeaux.
Selected Works / Œuvres Choisis 1979 – 1982. National Gallery of Canada, Ottawa.
Mexico 1979. Stedelijk Van Abbemuseum, Eindhoven.

1983
Touchstones. Text: Michael Craig-Martin. Arnolfini, Bristol.
Fango, Pietri, Legni. Galleria Tucci Russo, Turin.
Countless Stones. Stedelijk Van Abbemuseum, Eindhoven.
Planes of Vision. Ottenhausen Verlag, Aachen.

1984
Richard Long. Century Cultural Foundation, Tokyo.
River Avon Mud Works. Orchard Gallery, Londonderry.
Mud Hand Prints. Coracle Press, London.
Sixteen Works. Anthony d'Offay, London.

1985
Il Luogo Buono. Text in Italian and English. Padiglione d'Arte Contemporanea, Milan.
Richard Long. Fonds Régional d'Art Contemporain Aquitaine, Bordeaux.
Lines of Time / Tijdlijnen. Text in English and Dutch. Stichting Edy de Wilde Lezing / Openbaar Kunstbezit, Amsterdam.

1986
Piedras. Text in Spanish. Palacio de Cristal, Madrid.
Richard Long. Text: Rudi Fuchs. The Solomon R. Guggenheim Museum / Thames & Hudson, New York.

1987
Stone Water Miles. Text in French. Musée Rath, Geneva.
Out of the Wind. Donald Young Gallery, Chicago.
Dust Dobros Desert Flowers. The Lapis Press, Venice.

1988
Old World New World. Separate English and German editions. Neue Galerie Sammlung Ludwig, Aachen.

1989
Angel Flying too Close to the Ground. Kunstverein St. Gallen.
Surf Roar. La Jolla Museum of Contemporary Art, California.

1990
Sur la Route. Text in French. Musée départemental de Rochechouart.
Nile, Papers of River Muds. The Lapis Press, Los Angeles.

1991
Labyrinth. Städtische Galerie im Städel, Frankfurt.
Walking in Circles. Text: Hamish Fulton and Anne Seymour; interview: Richard Cork. The South Bank Centre, London

1992
Mountains and Waters. Anthony d'Offay Gallery, London.

1993
River to River. Text in French. ARC Musée de l'Art Moderne de la Ville de Paris.
Mountains and Waters. Special edition with print. Anthony d'Offay Gallery, London.

1994
Richard Long. Text in English and German. Kunstsammlung Nordrhein-Westfalen, Düsseldorf.
Richard Long. Separate English and Italian editions. Palazzo delle Esposizione, Rome.
No Where. The Pier Arts Centre, Stromness.
Richard Long, São Paulo Bienal 1994. The British Council, London.

1995
Walking, Mud, Stones…. Anthony d'Offay, London.

1996
Sangyo Suigyo. Text in Japanese, loose booklet in English. Setagaya Art Museum, Tokyo / The National Museum of Modern Art, Kyoto.

Circles, Cycles, Mud, Stones. Contemporary Arts Museum, Houston.
Dolomite Stones. Text in English, German and Italian. AR/Ge Kunst, Bolzano.
Dartmoor Time. Spacex Gallery, Exeter.

1997
Wind Circle, Memory Sticks. Wilhelm Lehmbruck Museum, Duisburg.
A Road from the Past to the Future. Text: John Haldane. The Crawford Arts Centre, St. Andrews.
A Walk across England. Thames & Hudson, London.
From Time to Time. Cantz Verlag, Ostfildern.

1998
Mirage. Phaidon Press, London.

1999
Every Grain of Sand. Text in German and English. Kunstverein Hannover, Hanover.
Being in the Moment. Text: Richard Long. Museum Kurhaus Kleve, Cleves.
Spanish Stones. Text by Gloria Moure. Édiciones Polígrafa, Barcelona.
Selected Walks 1979 – 1996. Centre for Artists' Books, Edinburgh.

2000
Richard Long in Leuk, Switzerland 2000. Stiftung Schloss Leuk.
Adamello Walk. Text in English and Italian. Museo d'Arte Moderna e Contemporanea di Trento e Rovereto, Trento.

2001
Midday. Text in German. Museum Kurhaus Kleve, Cleves.

2002
Richard Long – A Moving World. Tate St. Ives, Cornwall.

AUDIO, FILM AND VIDEO

1969
Land Art. Richard Long: Walking a Straight 10 Mile Line Forward and Back Shooting every Half Mile. Berlin, Fernsehgalerie Gerry Schum. 6 minutes, 33 seconds.

1982
Omnibus. BBC television, autumn 1982. 22 minutes.

1984
Four Mud Works, Ireland, Summer 1984. A video by Denny Long. 44 minutes.

1985
Richard Long, in conversation with William Furlong, London, February 1984. Audio Arts. 58 minutes.

1987
A Round of Desert Flowers: Straight Version / Bottle Neck Dobro. Music: Richard Long; dobro: Simon Childs. A 45 RPM record by Audio Arts, London, for 'Dust Dobro Desert Flowers'. 6 minutes, 20 seconds.

1988
Stones and Flies: Richard Long in the Sahara. A film by Philip Haas. A Methodact Production for The Arts Council of Great Britain in cooperation with Channel 4 Television, HPS Films Berlin, Centre Pompidou, La Sept, CNAP and WDR. London, Arts Council Video. 38 minutes.

PUBLIC COLLECTIONS
a selection.

Australia
Adelaide, Art Gallery of Victoria.
Canberra, National Gallery of Australia.

Austria
Vienna, Museum des 20. Jahrhunderts.

Belgium
Brussels, Museum voor Moderne Kunst.
Ghent, Museum van Hedendaagse Kunst.

Canada
Ottawa, National Gallery of Canada / Galerie nationale du Canada.
Toronto, Art Gallery of Ontario.

Denmark
Humlebæck, Louisiana Museum.

Finland
Helsinki, The Museum of the Ateneum.
Helsinki, Museum of Contemporary Art.

France
Bignan, Domaine de Kerguehennec.
Bordeaux, capcMusée d'Art Contemporain.
Epinal, Musée départemental de Vosges.
Nîmes, Carré d'Art.
Paris, Centre Georges Pompidou.
Paris, Musée d'Art Moderne de la Ville de Paris.
Rochechouart, Musée départemental de Rochechouart.

Germany
Berlin, Hamburger Bahnhof.
Duisburg, Wilhelm Lehmbruck Museum.
Cleves, Museum Kurhaus Kleve.
Cologne, Museum Ludwig.
Krefeld, Museum Haus Lange.
Mannheim, Städtische Kunsthalle.
Mönchengladbach, Städtisches Museum.
Wuppertal, Von der Heydt-Museum.

Great Britain
Bristol, Bristol City Museum & Art Gallery.
Edinburgh, Scottish National Gallery of Modern Art.
Leeds, Leeds City Art Gallery.
London, Arts Council of Great Britain.
London, Tate Gallery.
East Wintersloe, Roche Court, New Art Centre Sculpture Park & Gallery.
Southampton, Southampton City Art Gallery.
Swindon Art Gallery.

Ireland
Dublin, Irish Museum of Modern Art.

Italy
Turin, Castello di Rivoli.
Vinadio, Forte di Vinadio.

Japan
Hiroshima, City Museum of Contemporary Art.
Naoshima Contemporary Art Museum.
Tokyo, Museum of Contemporary Art.
Tokyo International Forum.
Tokyo Metropolitan Museum.

Netherlands
Amsterdam, Stedelijk Museum.
The Hague, Gemeentemuseum
Eindhoven, Stedelijk Van Abbemuseum.
Enschede, Rijksmuseum Twenthe.
Groningen, Groninger Museum.
Otterlo, Kröller-Müller Museum.
Rotterdam, Museum Boijmans-van Beuningen.
Tilburg, De Pont.

Portugal
Porto, Museu Serralves.

Sweden
Malmö Konsthall.
Stockholm, Moderna Museet.

Switzerland
Basel, Emanuel Hoffmann Collection.
Schaffhausen, Hallen für neue Kunst.
Zürich, The Crex Collection.

United States
Auckland Art Museum.
Cambridge, Fogg Art Museum.
Chicago, The Art Institute of Chicago.
Cleveland Museum of Art.
Dallas Museum of Art.
Detroit Institute of Arts.
Fort Worth, Modern Art Museum.
Houston, Museum of Fine Arts.
Marfa, The Chinati Foundation.
Minneapolis, Walker Art Center.
New York, The Solomon R. Guggenheim Museum.
New York, The Museum of Modern Art.
Philadelphia Museum of Art.
Pittsburgh, The Carnegie Museum of Art.
Saint Louis Art Museum.
San Fransisco Museum of Modern Art.
Seattle Art Museum.
Washington, National Gallery of Art.

PRIZES AND AWARDS

14 October 1988
Kunstpreis Aachen.

21 November 1989
Turner Prize.

15 June 1990
Chevalier dans l'Ordre des Arts et des Lettres.

10 July 1995
Doctor of Letters, honoris causa. University of Bristol.

13 January 1996
Wilhelm Lehmbruck-Preis, Duisburg.

PHOTO CREDITS

Page 198
Earthquake Circle
Galerie Tschudi Glarus 1991
© Mancia/Bodmer

Page 199
River Avon Mud Circle
Jean Bernier Athens 1992
© Dimitri Tamviskos

Page 210
Muddy Water Wall and Ring of White Marble
Galerie Tschudi Glarus 1993
© Mancia/Bodmer

Page 211
White Water Circle and Neandertal Line
Kunstsammlung Nordrhein-Westfalen Düsseldorf
1994
© Walter Klein

Page 213
Tierra del Fuego Circle Santa Cuz Circle
Chubut Circle
Sperone Westwater New York 1997
© Tom Powel

Page 214
Red Mud Circle
Palazzo delle Esposizioni Rome 1994
© Enzo Ricci

Page 215
Romulus Circle and Remus Circle
Palazzo delle Esposizioni Rome 1994
© Enzo Ricci

Page 216
Rome Circle
Palazzo delle Esposizioni Rome 1994
© Enzo Ricci

Pages 218–219
Muddy Water Circle
Palazzo delle Esposizioni Rome 1994
© Enzo Ricci

Page 220
Red And Grey Mud Wall
Tucci Russo Studio per l'Arte Contemporanea
Torre Pellice Italy 1994
© Paulo Mussat Sartor

Page 221
White River Line
São Paulo Bienal Brazil 1994
© Eduardo Ortege

Page 227
Hemisphere Circle
The Tokyo Forum Tokyo 1996
© Sadamu Saito

Page 232
Glarus Arc and Glarus Line
Galerie Tschudi Glarus 1996
© Mancia/Bodmer

Page 233
Berlin Circle
Hamburger Bahnhof Museum für Gegenwart
Berlin 1996
© Jens Ziehe

Page 234
Circle of Life
Spazio Zero Palermo 1997
© Shoba

Page 236–237
Black White Blue Purple Circle
Galerie Tschudi Glarus 1998
© Mancia/Bodmer

Pages 238–239
Black White Green Pink Purple Circle
Galerie Tschudi Glarus 1998
© Mancia/Bodmer

Page 240
Periphery Stones
Orangerie Kunstverein Hannover 1999
© Raimund Zakowski

Page 241
White Water Lines
Kunstverein Hannover 1999
© Raimund Zakowski

Page 244
Red Mud Ellipse
Tucci Russo Studio per l'Arte Contemporanea
Torre Pellice Italy 1998
© Enzo Ricci

Page 249
Energy Axis
Galeria Mário Sequeira Braga Portugal 1999
© Gustavo de Almeida Ribeiro

Page 254
River Avon Mud Arc
Bilbao Guggenheim 2000
© Erika Barahona Ede FMGB Guggenheim Bilbao

Page 257
Bilbao Circle
Bilbao Guggenheim 2000
© Erika Barahona Ede FMGB Guggenheim Bilbao

Page 258
Rhône Valley Mud Hand Circles
Schloss Leuk Switzerland 2000
© Thomas Andenmatten

Page 259
Rhône Valley Stones Spiral
Schloss Leuk Switzerland 2000
© Thomas Andenmatten

Page 267
Waterfall Line 2000 and Red Slate Circle 1987
Tate Modern London 2000
© Marcus Leigh

Page 268
Basalt Ellipse
Museum Kurhaus Kleve 2001
© Werner J. Hannappel

Pages 270–1
Making Fingerprint Stones
Southern California 1998
© Jerry Sohn

Pages 278–9
Making River Avon Mud Works on River Avon
Driftwood
Galerie Tschudi Glarus Switzerland 2000
© Jerry Sohn

Page 282
Following Thunder Tranquillity 2001
Galeria Mário Sequeira Braga Portugal 2001
© Xavier Antunes

Page 284
Installation Views Museum Kurhaus Kleve 2001
© Annegret Gossens

Page 285
River Avon Mud and China Clay Wall 2001
© Werner J. Hannappel

Pages 286–287
Forte di Vinadio Circle Italy 2001
© Werner J. Hannappel

Page 288
Heaven
Galerie Tschudi Glarus 2002
© Mancia/Bodmer

Page 289
Earth
Galerie Tschudi Glarus 2002
© Mancia/Bodmer

Page 291
Heaven and Earth Circle
Galerie Tschudi Glarus 2002
© Mancia/Bodmer

MAPS

Page 83
No Where
Scotland 1993

Page 99
Four Days and Four Circles
England 1994

Page 109
Concentric Days
Scotland 1996

Reproduced from the Ordnance Survey map with
the permission of Her Majesty's Stationery Office
© Crown Copyright MC 100013113

323

INDEX

Figures in *italics* refer to works discussed in
the Foreword, in Notes on Works 2000–2001,
a talk of 1997, and in essays.

First published in the United Kingdom in 2002 by Thames & Hudson Ltd, 181A High Holborn, London WC1V 7QX

First published in hardcover in the United States of America in 2002 by Thames & Hudson Inc., 500 Fifth Avenue, New York, New York 10110

Publication organized by Herman Lelie
Design Richard Long and Herman Lelie
Text set by Stefania Bonelli

British Library Cataloguing-in-Publication Data
A catalogue record for this book is available from the British Library

ISBN 0-500-51066-0

Library of Congress Catalog Card Number 2002103214

Printed and bound in Great Britain by St Ives Westerham Press

Endpapers: LIMESTONE, DRAWING ONE AND TWO, 2001

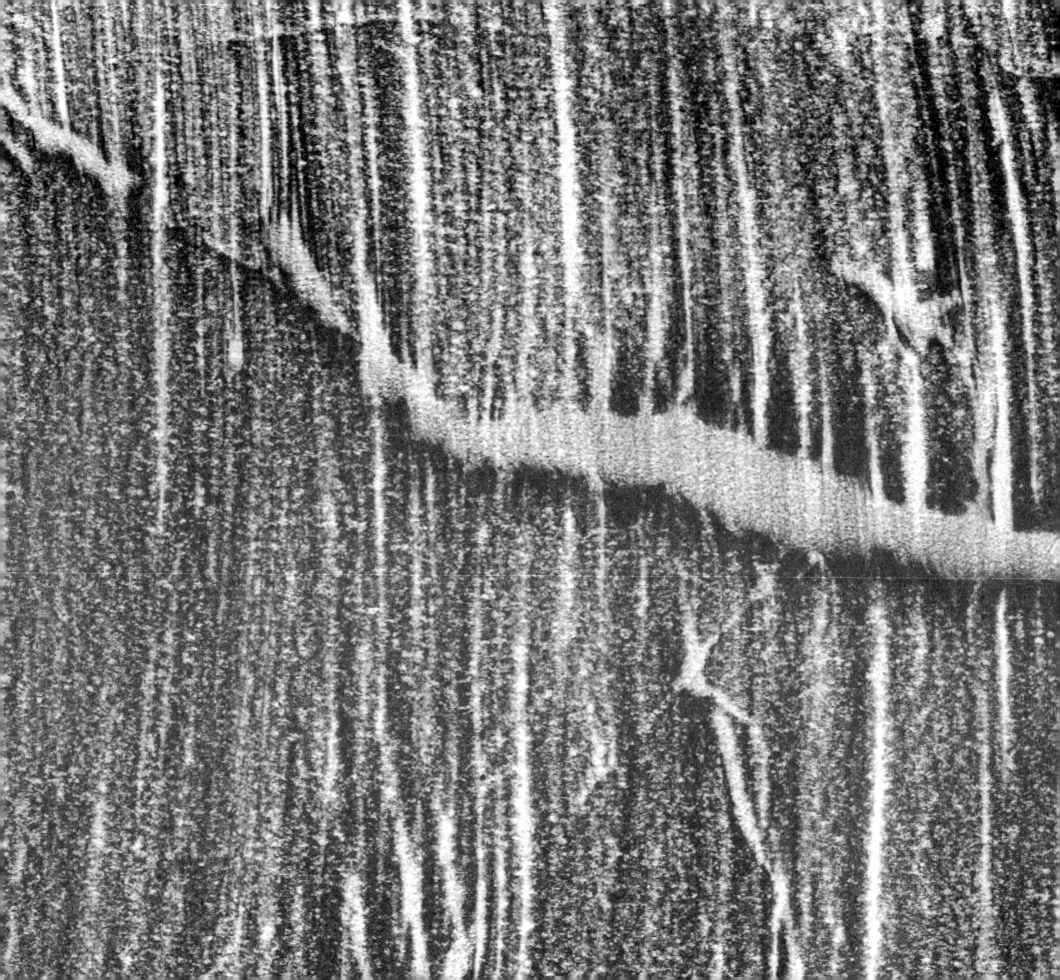